Voices from Primary Sources: World History

Krichak

Unit 1: Understanding Basic Documents

Unit 2: Finding the Voice

Unit 3: Listening on Your Own

Kubat (handwritten)

Unit 4: Test Practice with Document-Based Questions

Introduction ··

For many students, history is a boring slog through the past. They have to read lifeless renditions of events, and they have to memorize dates and places. Indeed, some historical dates and places are utterly important. Unfortunately, this typical approach to history overlooks the fact that we are all a part of history on a daily basis—and sometimes what we witness becomes historically important. Primary sources are often eyewitness accounts of historical events. These accounts can make history come alive for the student.

This book balances a generous number of primary sources with secondary sources such as charts, graphs, time lines, and historical perspectives by more modern writers. It will help students improve their reading comprehension and social studies skills. The book is excellent practice for the increased use of document-based questions (DBQs) on major tests.

Document-Based Questions (DBQs)

DBQs are an important part of today's educational environment. To understand their world better, students must be able to analyze information as well as the documents that contain that information. Studying and analyzing each group of documents will allow students to develop their critical-thinking skills. Increasingly, social studies exams are using DBQs to assess competence in writing and social studies. This book is designed to help students succeed at answering document-based questions and essays.

Organization

The book uses a scaffolded process to acquaint the student with DBQs.

- **Unit 1: Understanding Basic Documents** introduces the most common types of documents used in testing. Student responses to exercise questions are factual.

- **Unit 2: Finding the Voice** provides more detailed steps to using documents. Student responses to exercise questions are factual and critical.

- **Unit 3: Listening on Your Own** gives students more extensive practice with documents. After studying tip boxes, students examine documents on their own. Student responses to exercise questions are factual and critical. This unit also includes a practice DBQ test and a sample top score essay.

- **Unit 4: Test Practice with DBQs** includes six practice tests with various documents.

- Other features include an essay scoring rubric and an answer key.

- Beginning on page 119 are four worksheets that you can distribute to students to help them work with different kinds of documents.

Standards

One basic standard of social studies is that students use various intellectual skills to show their understanding of major ideas, eras, themes, and turning points in the history of the world. To demonstrate this understanding, students should:

- use primary and secondary records to analyze major events that shaped the world;

- appreciate historical events through the experiences of those who were present;

- explore world cultures and civilizations by identifying key ideas, beliefs, values, and traditions;

- explain the significance of historical evidence; judge the importance and reliability of evidence; and understand the importance of changing interpretations of history.

Additional Lessons Using Primary Sources

Two government Web sites, the Library of Congress and the National Archives and Records Administration, provide extensive resources for teachers and students. Both Web sites provide lesson plans for using primary documents in the study of history. These sites primarily focus on United States history but include documents relating to United States involvement in world affairs. You can visit these two Web sites at the links below.

Library of Congress:
http://memory.loc.gov/learn/lessons/primary.html

National Archives and Records Administration:
http://www.archives.gov/education/

Features ···

Unit 1 introduces the most common types of documents used in testing.

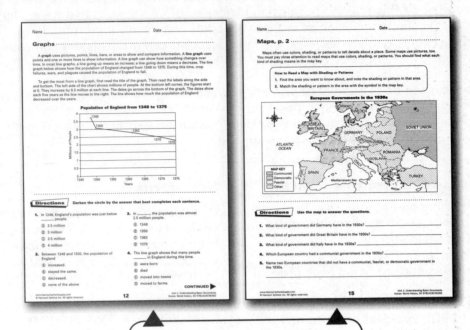

Student responses to exercise questions in this unit are factual.

Parts of the document are highlighted to aid student understanding.

Unit 2 gives more detailed steps to using documents.

Tips for approaching the documents are included.

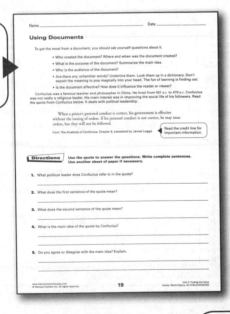

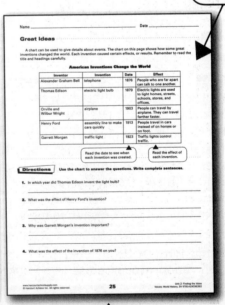

Student responses to exercise questions in this unit are factual and critical.

Unit 3 gives students more extensive practice with documents.

A tip box gives students hints on how to approach the document.

A credit line tells the source of the document.

Captions tell more about graphic images.

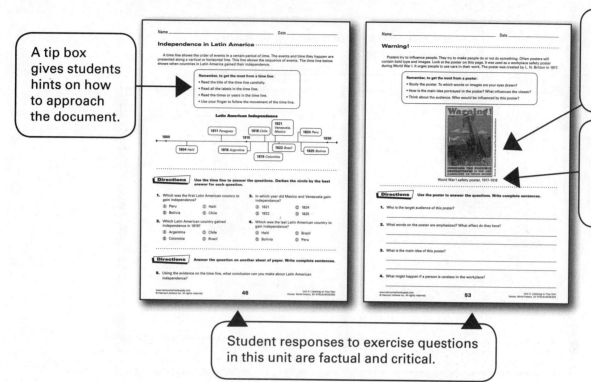

Student responses to exercise questions in this unit are factual and critical.

A practice test gives students a chance to deal with the testing situation without pressure.

A brief historical background gives students a foundation to understand the documents.

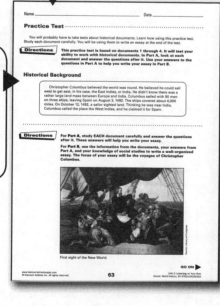

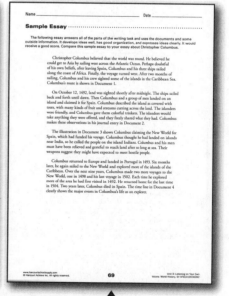

A sample essay shows students what is expected on a well-written essay.

Unit 4 includes six practice tests with various documents.

A practice test includes several different kinds of documents.

Brief background information is given for many documents.

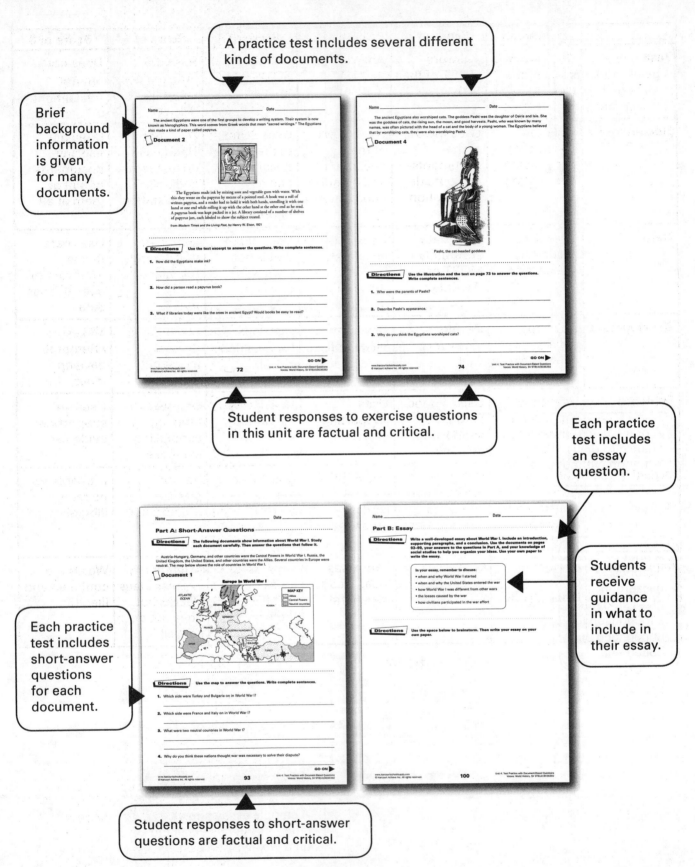

Student responses to exercise questions in this unit are factual and critical.

Each practice test includes an essay question.

Each practice test includes short-answer questions for each document.

Students receive guidance in what to include in their essay.

Student responses to short-answer questions are factual and critical.

Rubric for Document-Based Essays

	Score of 5	Score of 4	Score of 3	Score of 2	Score of 1	Score of 0
Task	Answers ALL parts of the task	Answers MOST of the task	Answers the task	Answers SOME of the task	Has very little understanding of the task	Does not answer the task
Documents	Uses the documents and outside information	Uses MOST of the documents and outside information	Uses SOME of the documents and outside information	Uses SOME of the documents and no outside information	Does not clearly use documents and only hints at them	Does not use any documents or hint at them at all
Data	Uses data accurately ALL of the time	Uses data accurately MOST of the time	Uses data accurately SOME of the time	Uses data that is not always relevant	Uses data that is rarely relevant	Uses data that is irrelevant or does not use data
Development	Develops ideas completely	Develops ideas very well	Develops ideas well	Develops ideas poorly	Attempts to develop ideas, but does not	Makes no attempt to develop ideas
Evidence	Uses much supporting evidence	Uses a good amount of supporting evidence	Uses supporting evidence	Uses SOME supporting evidence	Uses very little supporting evidence	Uses no supporting evidence
Organization	Has very good organization and strong development	Has good organization and good development	Has STRONG general plan of organization	Has WEAK general plan of organization	Has no plan of organization	Is unable to be read; illegible
Expression	Always expresses ideas clearly	Expresses ideas clearly MOST of the time	Expresses ideas clearly in general	Expresses ideas clearly SOME of the time	Attempts to express ideas clearly, but does not do so well	Words are confused and illegible

Scoring Rubric
Voices: World History, SV 9781419036392

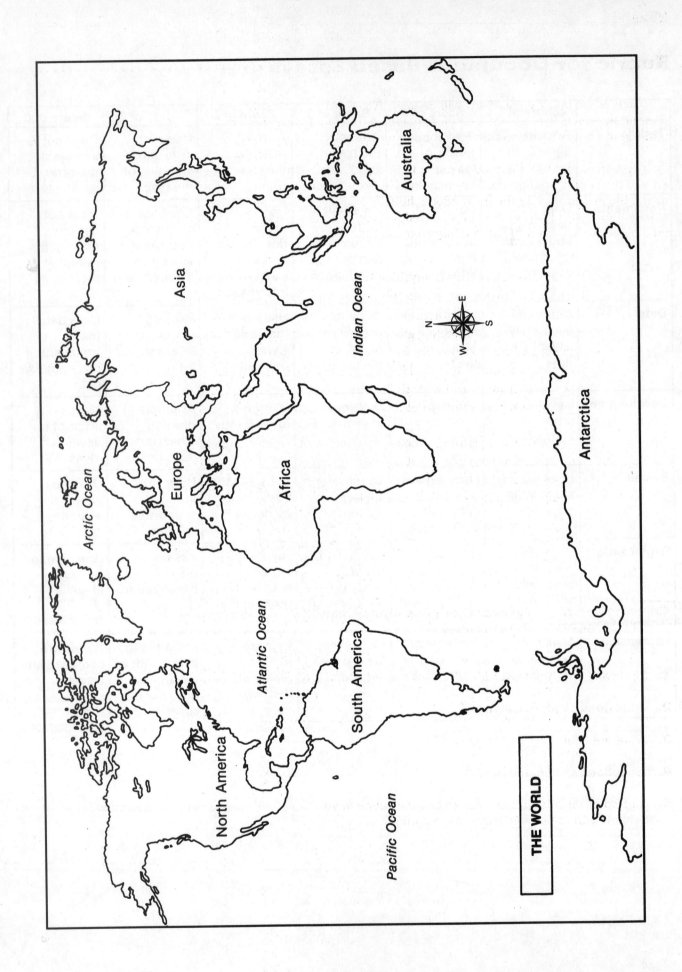

THE WORLD

World Map
Voices: World History, SV 9781419036392

Text ··

Much world history you learn will be in written form. You must read the **text** carefully to be sure you understand the meaning. You can't just glance at the words and hope to know what they mean. If you don't understand a word, you should look it up in a dictionary.

When the Industrial Revolution came to England in the 18th century, many factories were built in an area in the center of England. The machines in the factories burned coal, and soon the area became known as the Black Country. By the early 1800s, houses and any trees that remained were black with soot. The stars could not be seen in the sky, and people who lived there had short lifespans. James Nasmyth, an engineer who invented the steam hammer, visited the area in 1830.

> The Black Country is anything but picturesque. The earth seems to have been turned inside out. Its entrails are strewn about; nearly the entire surface of the ground is covered with cinder-heaps and mounds of scoriae. The coal, which has been drawn from below ground, is blazing on the surface. . . . By day and by night the country is glowing with fire, and the smoke of the ironworks hovers over it. There is a rumbling and clanking of iron forges and rolling mills. Workmen covered with smut, and with fierce white eyes, are seen moving about amongst the glowing iron and dull thud of forge-hammers.
>
> Amidst these flaming, smoky, clanging works, I beheld the remains of what had once been happy farmhouses, now ruined and deserted. . . . They had in former times been surrounded by clumps of trees but only the skeletons of them remained, dilapidated, black, and lifeless.
>
> from *James Nasmyth: Engineer, An Autobiography*, Chapter 9

···

Directions   **Answer these questions on another sheet of paper. Use a dictionary if necessary.**

1. Circle any unfamiliar words. Which words did you circle?

2. What does *picturesque* mean?

3. What are "entrails" and "scoriae"?

4. What does *dilapidated* mean?

5. A good description allows you to see the scene in your mind. What words or images does Nasmyth use to allow you to see the scene in your mind?

Charts ···

A **chart** gives information in the form of a picture or list. Charts provide much information in a small space. They make it easy to compare information. A chart lists a group of facts. Charts help you learn facts quickly. Read this chart to learn about the Punic Wars. The Punic Wars were a series of conflicts for control of the Mediterranean Sea and lands around it.

The Punic Wars

Punic War	Dates Fought	Reason Fought	Results of War
First Punic War	264 B.C.–241 B.C.	Rome and Carthage wanted control of the Mediterranean Sea.	• Romans won the war and gained Sicily. • Carthage paid Rome for damages.
Second Punic War	218 B.C.–202 B.C.	Carthage and Rome wanted to control lands in Spain.	• Rome defeated Hannibal and gained land in Spain. • Rome also received money and ships from Carthage.
Third Punic War	149 B.C.–146 B.C.	Carthage fought against the agreement resulting from the Second Punic War.	• Rome won and gained control of the Mediterranean Sea. • Carthage was destroyed.

In the chart, look at the label at the top of each **column** of figures. The second column says *Dates Fought*. You can see that the First Punic War was fought from 264 B.C. to 241 B.C. (Years B.C. get smaller as they move forward.) The third column tells why each war was fought, and the fourth column tells the results of the war. If you read left to right along the **row**, you find out details about each of the Punic Wars.

· ·

Directions | Use the chart to answer the questions. Write complete sentences.

1. Which was the shortest Punic War?

_____

2. Which Punic War was fought to control lands in Spain?

_____

3. What was one result of the Third Punic War?

_____

10

Name _____   Date _____

Time Lines ··

A **time line** is a kind of chart. As you remember, a chart arranges facts in a way that makes them easy to read and understand. A time line shows the order of events along a vertical or horizontal line.

- Read the title of the time line carefully.

- Read the years in the time line. Then read all the labels in the time line.

- Use your finger to follow the movement of the time line.

- Be sure you know what information you need and what information the time line gives.

Look at the time line below. This time line covers the Middle Ages, the Renaissance, the Reformation, and the early years of the Industrial Revolution. A lot happened during all those years! Notice how the time line makes all the information easy to understand.

Important Events: A.D. 476–1764

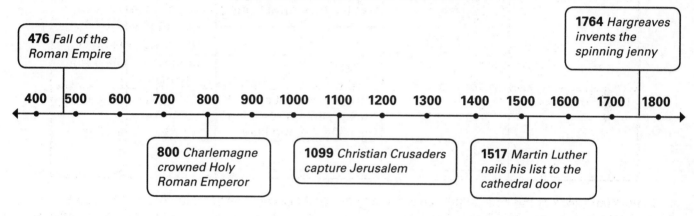

Directions / Use the time line to answer each question. Write complete sentences.

1. According to the time line, what happened in 476?

_____

2. When did Charlemagne become Emperor of the Holy Roman Empire?

_____

3. When did Christian Crusaders capture Jerusalem?

_____

4. The Muslims recaptured Jerusalem in 1187. Mark the date on the time line and write a label for the event.

5. How many years went by between Charlemagne being crowned emperor and Martin Luther nailing his list to the cathedral door?

_____

Unit 1: Understanding Basic Documents
Voices: World History, SV 9781419036392

Graphs ···

A **graph** uses pictures, points, lines, bars, or areas to show and compare information. A **line graph** uses points and one or more lines to show information. A line graph can show how something changes over time. In most line graphs, a line going up means an increase; a line going down means a decrease. The line graph below shows how the population of England changed from 1348 to 1375. During this time, crop failures, wars, and plagues caused the population of England to fall.

To get the most from a line graph, first read the title of the graph. Then read the labels along the side and bottom. The left side of the chart shows millions of people. At the bottom left corner, the figures start at 0. They increase by 0.5 million at each line. The dates go across the bottom of the graph. The dates show each five years as the line moves to the right. The line shows how much the population of England decreased over the years.

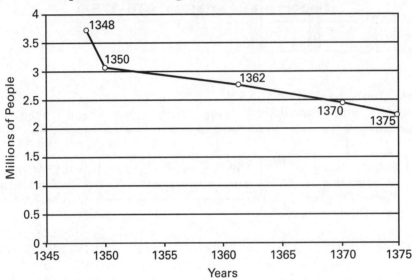

Population of England from 1348 to 1375

···

Directions | Darken the circle by the answer that best completes each sentence.

1. In 1348, England's population was just below _____ people.

   Ⓐ 2.5 million

   Ⓑ 3 million

   Ⓒ 3.5 million

   Ⓓ 4 million

2. Between 1348 and 1350, the population of England

   Ⓐ increased.

   Ⓑ stayed the same.

   Ⓒ decreased.

   Ⓓ none of the above

3. In _____, the population was almost 2.5 million people.

   Ⓐ 1348

   Ⓑ 1350

   Ⓒ 1362

   Ⓓ 1370

4. The line graph shows that many people _____ in England during this time.

   Ⓐ were born

   Ⓑ died

   Ⓒ moved into towns

   Ⓓ moved to farms

CONTINUED ▶

Graphs, p. 2 ·····································

Another kind of graph is a **bar graph**. A bar graph shows how figures compare in size. The bar graph below compares the production of silver and gold in Mexico between 1877 and 1908. The shading on the bars helps you see which bars represent which metal. The numbers on the left side show the value of the metals in millions of pesos.

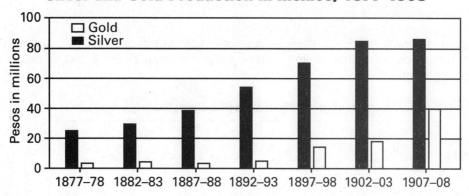

Silver and Gold Production in Mexico, 1877–1908

A **pie graph** or **circle graph** uses wedge-shaped "slices" to compare a part to the whole. The whole is always 100%. Each number becomes a slice of the whole pie. The pie graph on this page tells about the followers of religions in Europe.

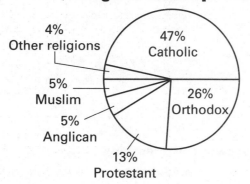

Religions in Europe Today

Directions Use the two graphs on this page to answer the questions. Write complete sentences on another sheet of paper.

1. What was the value of the gold produced in Mexico in 1907–1908?

2. In which years was the value of silver about 30 million pesos?

3. Which metal—silver or gold—had the greater value during the time shown on the graph?

4. Which religion do the most people in Europe believe in today?

5. What percent of the people in Europe are Muslims?

Name _____   Date _____

Maps ···

A **map** is a drawing of a place or area. Maps can tell about the boundaries of places, such as states or countries. They can tell about the landscape, the climate, the population, or many other things. All maps have a title to tell what the map shows.

A **political map** shows the boundaries of nations. Often, the capital city and major cities of a nation are included on a political map. The map below shows the Middle East today. It also includes information on a historical region called the Fertile Crescent.

Symbols on the map stand for real things. To learn what the symbols stand for, read the **map key**, or **legend**. A map may include a distance scale to tell how far apart places are. Most maps also have a **compass rose** to tell directions.

The Middle East

| **Directions** | Use the map to answer the questions. |

1. Which city is the capital of Egypt? _____

2. What body of water forms Saudi Arabia's western border? _____

3. Which city is nearer Baghdad: Kuwait City or Khartoum? About how far in miles is the nearer city from

Baghdad? _____

4. What is the distance in kilometers from Riyadh to Amman? _____

5. The Fertile Crescent was the location of several early civilizations. Between which two rivers was the Fertile Crescent located?

_____

6. In which present-day countries is much of the Fertile Crescent located?

_____

CONTINUED ▶

Maps, p. 2 ··

Maps often use colors, shading, or patterns to tell details about a place. Some maps use pictures, too. You must pay close attention to read maps that use colors, shading, or patterns. You should find what each kind of shading means in the map key.

> **How to Read a Map with Shading or Patterns**
>
> 1. Find the area you want to know about, and note the shading or pattern in that area.
>
> 2. Match the shading or pattern in the area with the symbol in the map key.

European Governments in the 1930s

Directions | Use the map to answer the questions.

1. What kind of government did Germany have in the 1930s? _____

2. What kind of government did Great Britain have in the 1930s? _____

3. What kind of government did Italy have in the 1930s? _____

4. Which European country had a communist government in the 1930s? _____

5. Name two European countries that did not have a communist, fascist, or democratic government in the 1930s.

_____

15

Posters ···

A **poster** is a large graphic card or notice that is displayed in a public place. Posters can be used to advertise products. They can tell about artistic performances or candidates for election. They can urge people to take some action. Most posters include both words and pictures.

The words in biggest letters on the poster are usually the most important. A poster usually has pictures, too. A picture of a product, performer, or candidate might be on the poster. The pictures might be symbolic images. What does the loaf of bread symbolize?

During wars, citizens are often asked to make sacrifices to help the war effort. The poster below wants people in the United States to save food to help win World War I.

A poster urging conservation during World War I, 1918

···

Directions Use the poster to answer the questions.

1. What does the poster tell people to do?

_____

2. What do you think the loaf of bread symbolizes?

_____

3. Would this poster make you support the war effort? Tell why or why not.

_____

_____

Name _____   Date _____

Photographs ···

A picture is worth a thousand words, the old saying goes. **Photographs** can provide a record of history, both personal and public. Photographs can show us the history of the world. They can freeze actions in time. The photograph below was taken during World War II. It shows the first German bombing raid on London, England, in September 1940.

To gain the most from a photograph, first pay attention to the images. What is in the center of the picture? What is in the foreground? What is in the background? Notice the use of light and dark in the photograph. What mood does the photographer establish?

A photograph may also have a **caption**. The caption gives written information about the photograph. What is the caption of this photograph?

Source: National Archives and Records Administration

Bombing raid on London, September 7, 1940

· ·

Directions   **Use the photograph and caption to answer the questions.**

1. When was this photograph taken? _____

2. What are the main images in the photograph? _____

_____

3. How does the photograph make you feel?

_____

_____

_____

Name _____ Date _____

Political Cartoons ··

A political, or editorial, cartoon is an illustration that contains a social or political message. The cartoon tries to make a point. **Political cartoons** usually require the reader to have some knowledge of current events.

Study the cartoon below. Political cartoonists often label things in the cartoon. Notice that the boxing glove is labeled, and the man has swastikas on his collar. Political cartoons may also have captions. This cartoon was drawn by Charles Alston in 1943. It urges recycling during World War II.

Source: National Archives and Records Administration

··

| **Directions** | Use the political cartoon to answer the questions. |

1. Who does the man in the cartoon represent?

_____

2. What country did he lead during World War II?

_____

3. What is the caption of this political cartoon? What does the caption mean? In other words, what is the main idea of this cartoon?

_____

_____

_____

Using Documents ·

To get the most from a document, you should ask yourself questions about it.

- Who created the document? Where and when was the document created?

- What is the purpose of the document? Summarize the main idea.

- Who is the audience of the document?

- Are there any unfamiliar words? Underline them. Look them up in a dictionary. Don't expect the meaning to pop magically into your head. The fun of learning is finding out.

- Is the document effective? How does it influence the reader or viewer?

Confucius was a famous teacher and philosopher in China. He lived from 551 B.C. to 479 B.C. Confucius was not really a religious leader. His main interest was in improving the social life of his followers. Read the quote from Confucius below. It deals with political leadership.

> When a prince's personal conduct is correct, his government is effective without the issuing of orders. If his personal conduct is not correct, he may issue orders, but they will not be followed.

from *The Analects of Confucius*, Chapter 9, translated by James Legge

Read the credit line for important information.

· ·

Directions Use the quote to answer the questions. Write complete sentences. Use another sheet of paper if necessary.

1. What political leader does Confucius refer to in the quote?

_____

2. What does the first sentence of the quote mean?

_____

3. What does the second sentence of the quote mean?

_____

4. What is the main idea of the quote by Confucius?

_____

_____

5. Do you agree or disagree with the main idea? Explain.

_____

_____

History Repeats Itself ··

Excavations at the ancient Babylonian city of Ur revealed clay tablets from around 1800 B.C. The people in this region were some of the first to use writing. Some of the tablets told of everyday life in the city. The excerpt below tells of the daily life of a Sumerian schoolboy.

> Arriving at school in the morning I recited my tablet, ate my lunch, prepared my new tablet, wrote it, finished it, then they assigned me my oral work. . . . When school was dismissed, I went home, entered the house, and found my father sitting there. I told my father of my written work, then recited my tablet to him, and my father was delighted.
>
> Anonymous, 1780 B.C.

· ·

Directions / Use the excerpt to answer the questions. Write complete sentences.

1. When was the tablet written?

_____

2. What does *anonymous* mean?

_____

3. How is the schoolday described similar to or different from your day at school?

_____

_____

_____

_____

_____

_____

_____

_____

_____

_____

Witch Trials ·

From about 1400 to 1700, hundreds of thousands of people in Europe and North America were accused of being witches. Most of the accused were women. Even though trials were held, most of the accused were found guilty of witchcraft. Then they were killed. Many were burned at the stake. Others were drowned.

One test for a witch was the water test. The accused woman was tied up and thrown into a body of water. If she sank into the water and drowned, she was not a witch. If she did not sink and drown, she was considered a witch and killed.

The diary excerpt below tells of a witchcraft trial in Essex, England, in 1699.

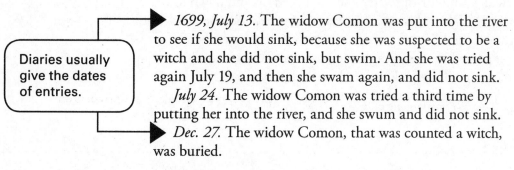

Diaries usually give the dates of entries.

1699, July 13. The widow Comon was put into the river to see if she would sink, because she was suspected to be a witch and she did not sink, but swim. And she was tried again July 19, and then she swam again, and did not sink.

July 24. The widow Comon was tried a third time by putting her into the river, and she swum and did not sink.

Dec. 27. The widow Comon, that was counted a witch, was buried.

from Diary of John Bufton, 1699

· ·

Directions   **Use the diary entry to answer the questions.**

1. Who is accused of being a witch? _____

2. When was she first given the water test? _____

3. When was she last given the water test? _____

4. What is the meaning of the entry on December 27?

_____

_____

5. Do you think the water test is a reliable way to tell if a person is a witch? Explain.

_____

_____

_____

_____

Ducking Stool ···

In the 17th century, women who were scolds were often punished publicly. A scold is someone who is noisy or quarrelsome. The punishment was to plunge the scold repeatedly into the water using a ducking stool.

Look up any unfamiliar words.

The trebuchet, or trebucket, was a . . . simple form of a ducking machine consisting of a short post set at the water's edge with a long beam resting on it like a see-saw. By a simple contrivance it could be swung round parallel to the bank, and the culprit tied in the chair affixed to one end. Then she could be swung out over the water and see-sawed up and down into the water. When this machine was not in use, it was secured to a stump or bolt in the ground by a padlock because when left free it proved too tempting and convenient an opportunity for tormenting village children to duck each other.

from *Curious Punishments of Bygone Days*, by Alice Morse Earle, 1896

· ·

Directions   Use the text to answer the questions. Write complete sentences.

1. Did you look up any words in this passage? Which words? What do they mean?

_____

_____

2. What form of ducking machine is described in the passage?

_____

_____

3 Why was the ducking machine locked up when not in use?

_____

_____

CONTINUED ▶

Ducking Stool, p. 2 ···

A picture can sometimes make text easier to understand. Study the picture below. Then reread the description on page 22. Does the picture help you to understand the machine?

Source: *Curious Punishments of Bygone Days*, illustration by Frank Hazenplug, 1896

···

Directions   **Use the illustration to answer the questions. Write complete sentences. Use another sheet of paper.**

1. Who drew the illustration of the ducking machine?

2. When was the illustration first published?

3. Do you think ducking was a good punishment for a scold? Tell why or why not.

4. Do you think punishments such as ducking should be used now? Explain.

5. Choose a misbehavior. Then write a punishment for that misbehavior.

www.harcourtschoolsupply.com
23
Unit 2: Finding the Voice
Voices: World History, SV 9781419036392

The World at War ·····························

A chart lists a group of facts. A chart can be used to classify information. Look at the chart below. It categorizes the main nations involved in World War II. The Allies and the Axis countries were actively fighting. The neutral countries were trying to stay out of the conflict.

Read the title to see what information the chart contains.

▶ **Nations at War**

Read the column headings to see what the information in the column refers to.

Allies	Axis Countries	Neutral Countries
United States	Germany	Switzerland
Great Britain	Italy	Sweden
France	Japan	Spain
Soviet Union		Portugal
China		Turkey
Australia		Ireland
Canada		
Mexico		

· ·

Directions   Use the chart to answer the questions. Write complete sentences.

1. Which was the largest group of nations?

_____

2. What does *neutral* mean? Name a neutral country from the chart.

_____

_____

3. Which three nations were called the Axis countries?

_____

_____

4. Name three countries that fought against Germany in World War II.

_____

_____

Great Ideas ·

A chart can be used to give details about events. The chart on this page shows how some great inventions changed the world. Each invention caused certain effects, or results. Remember to read the title and headings carefully.

American Inventions Change the World

Inventor	Invention	Date	Effect
Alexander Graham Bell	telephone	1876	People who are far apart can talk to one another.
Thomas Edison	electric light bulb	1879	Electric lights are used to light homes, streets, schools, stores, and offices.
Orville and Wilbur Wright	airplane	1903	People can travel by airplane. They can travel farther faster.
Henry Ford	assembly line to make cars quickly	1913	People travel in cars instead of on horses or on foot.
Garrett Morgan	traffic light	1923	Traffic lights control traffic.

Read the date to see when each invention was created.

Read the effect of each invention.

Directions   Use the chart to answer the questions. Write complete sentences.

1. In which year did Thomas Edison invent the light bulb?

_____

2. What was the effect of Henry Ford's invention?

_____

_____

3. Why was Garrett Morgan's invention important?

_____

_____

4. What was the effect of the invention of 1876 on you?

_____

_____

Eye-Openers ···

A time line shows the order of events in a certain period of time. The events and time they happen are presented along a vertical or horizontal line. This line shows the sequence of events. The time line below shows important events in optics.

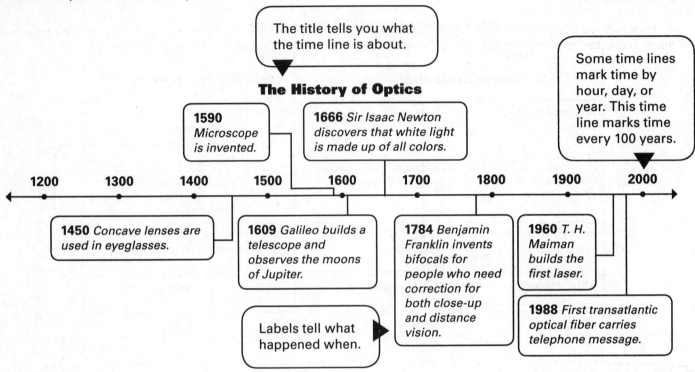

The title tells you what the time line is about.

Some time lines mark time by hour, day, or year. This time line marks time every 100 years.

The History of Optics

1590 *Microscope is invented.*

1666 *Sir Isaac Newton discovers that white light is made up of all colors.*

1200   1300   1400   1500   1600   1700   1800   1900   2000

1450 *Concave lenses are used in eyeglasses.*

1609 *Galileo builds a telescope and observes the moons of Jupiter.*

1784 *Benjamin Franklin invents bifocals for people who need correction for both close-up and distance vision.*

1960 *T. H. Maiman builds the first laser.*

1988 *First transatlantic optical fiber carries telephone message.*

Labels tell what happened when.

···

Directions   Use the time line to answer the questions. Write complete sentences.

1. When was the first laser built?

_____

2. What happened in optics history in 1666?

_____

3. Two important events occurred around 1600. What were the two events? Why do you think they were important?

_____

_____

_____

4. Are events easier to understand on a time line or in a paragraph of information? Explain.

_____

_____

_____

Name _____ Date _____

Burning Questions ··

A line graph shows how something changes over time. The line may go up and down to show increases or decreases. As always, read the title and labels carefully so you know what information the graph contains.

People have used different energy sources throughout history. The line graph on this page shows how many households in the United States burned wood as the main fuel from 1981 to 1990.

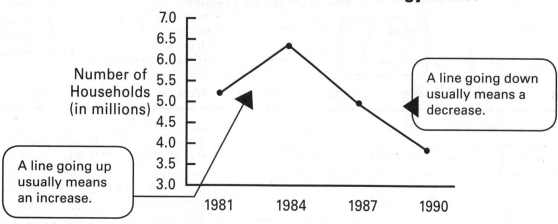

U.S. Households that Burn Wood as Main Energy Source

A line going up usually means an increase.

A line going down usually means a decrease.

Number of Households (in millions)

··

Directions | Use the graph to answer the questions. Write complete sentences.

1. In 1981, about how many U.S. households burned wood as the main fuel?

_____

2. In which year did the most households burn wood as the main fuel?

_____

3. After 1984, what happened to the number of households using wood?

_____

_____

4. Why do you think fewer households used wood as the main energy source?

_____

_____

_____

_____

Seeing Double ···

Sometimes a line graph has two lines. This kind of graph is called a double-line graph. Each line represents something different. The graph below shows population growth from 1960 to 2000. One line represents India. The second line represents China.

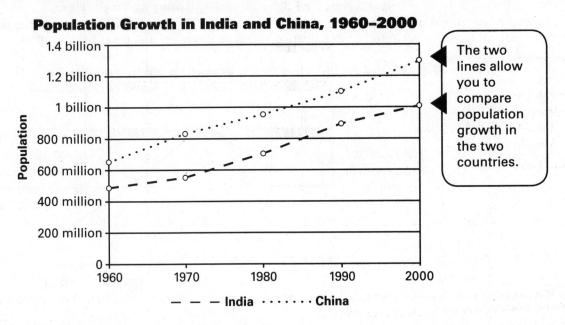

Population Growth in India and China, 1960–2000

The two lines allow you to compare population growth in the two countries.

— — India ······· China

···

Directions Use the graph to answer the questions. Write complete sentences.

1. What was the population of India in 1990?

_____

2. In what year did the population of China pass one billion?

_____

3. Does the graph ever show a decrease in population in the two countries?

_____

4. India's population reached one billion people by the year 2000. Do you think India's population will be above 1.5 billion by 2010? Use the information from the graph to explain your answer.

_____

_____

_____

Name _____ Date _____

African Kingdoms ·····································

A bar graph uses bars of different lengths to show facts. The bar graph below shows the greatest population of African kingdoms at the peak of their civilizations.

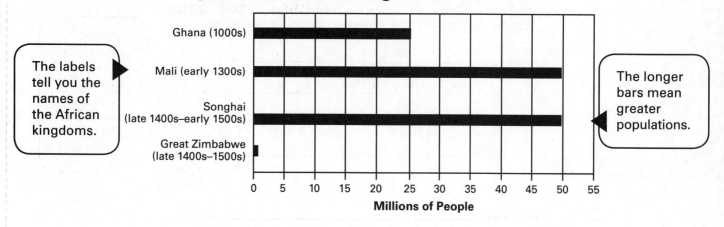

Populations of African Kingdoms at Their Peaks

The labels tell you the names of the African kingdoms.

The longer bars mean greater populations.

· ·

Directions | Use the graph to answer each question. Darken the circle by the best answer.

1. How many people might have lived in Ghana in the l000s?

   Ⓐ 1 million

   Ⓑ 20 million

   Ⓒ 25 million

   Ⓓ 50 million

2. About how many people lived in Mali when it was at its peak?

   Ⓐ 1 million

   Ⓑ 25 million

   Ⓒ 40 million

   Ⓓ 50 million

3. When did Songhai have about 50 million people?

   Ⓐ 1000s

   Ⓑ early 1300s

   Ⓒ late 1400s to early 1500s

   Ⓓ 2006

4. Which of these kingdoms had the smallest population at its peak?

   Ⓐ Ghana

   Ⓑ Mali

   Ⓒ Songhai

   Ⓓ Great Zimbabwe

Name _____ Date _____

Comparing Graphs ··

Sometimes you will have to compare two graphs to determine how changes have occurred. As you remember, a pie graph uses slices to equal 100%. The two pie graphs below show trade between the United States and Japan in 1997 and 2006. By comparing the two graphs, you can see changes in trade patterns.

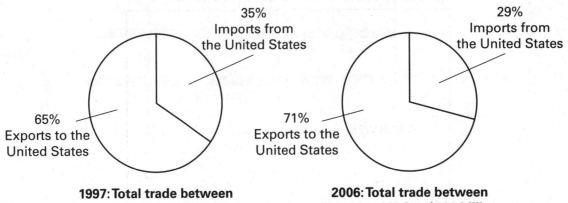

Trade Between the United States and Japan

35% Imports from the United States

65% Exports to the United States

1997: Total trade between Japan and U.S. = $187 billion

29% Imports from the United States

71% Exports to the United States

2006: Total trade between Japan and U.S. = $193 billion

··

| **Directions** | **Use the graphs to answer the questions.** |

1. In 1997, what percentage of the United States-Japanese trade was imports from the United States?

_____

2. In 1997, what percentage of the United States-Japanese trade was exports to the United States?

_____

3. Did trade between the United States and Japan increase or decrease between 1997 and 2006?

_____

4. Did imports and exports between the two nations change between 1997 and 2006? Explain.

_____

_____

_____

_____

_____

Name _____ Date _____

Resources ·

As you know, maps are a special kind of drawing of a place. Maps can show many types of information about a place. Maps can show borders, landforms, rivers, and routes. They can show population and precipitation. They can tell where events happened or where places are located. They can show the resources in a place at a particular time in history. Learning to use maps well can help you find your way around the world. Maps can also help you learn more about history.

The title tells you what the map is about.

The map key may include shading or symbols.

The compass rose tells directions.

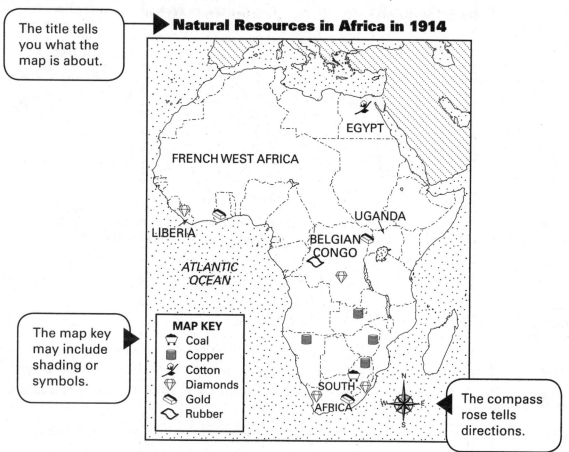

Natural Resources in Africa in 1914

· ·

Directions Use the map to answer the questions.

1. What year does this map refer to? _____

2. Which natural resource could be found in Egypt? _____

3. In which African countries could diamonds be found? _____

4. Which country in Africa had the most natural resources? _____

5. If you traveled from Uganda to Liberia, which direction would you go? _____

Unit 2: Finding the Voice
Voices: World History, SV 9781419036392

Name _____ Date _____

People and Places · · · · · · · · · · · · · · · · · · ·

At times you may be required to compare maps to draw conclusions. Some maps give information about how many people live in a place. Maps can also give information on reasons people might choose to live in a place. The maps on this page show the population and climate of Australia. Why might people in Australia live where they do?

Population Map of Australia   **Climate Map of Australia**

· ·

Directions   **Circle the compass rose and map key on each map. Then use the maps to answer the questions.**

1. What kind of climate does most of Australia have? _____

2. About how many people per square mile live near Alice Springs? _____

3. What kind of climate can be found around Darwin? _____

4. In which part of Australia do the most people live? _____

5. Why do you think most people choose to live in that part of Australia? Use evidence from both maps to explain.

_____

_____

_____

_____

Name _____ Date _____

Victims of War ···

Soldiers are not the only ones who suffer during war. Often the lives of civilians in war-torn areas are upset, too. Study the picture of these children in London, England, during World War II. The Germans started bombing London in September 1940.

To get the most from a photograph, you must pay careful attention to the details of the image. Are there important details in the background? What is shown in the center of the photograph? Is there a caption? What does it say?

Source: National Archives and Records Administration

London children in front of their bombed home, September 1940

···

Directions Use the photograph to answer the questions. Write complete sentences. Use another sheet of paper.

1. What is the central image in the photograph?

2. How do you think the children feel?

3. How does the photograph make you feel?

4. What would you do if your home had just been bombed?

5. Do you think a photograph can make you feel or think a certain way? Explain.

Name _____   Date _____

Buy Bonds · 35 · · · · · · · · · · · · · · · · ·

A poster tries to influence people. It can make people vote for a candidate or buy a certain product. Posters often have bright colors and bold images. The poster on page 35 was originally printed in color. The woman's robe was red, white, and blue. The shield and sword were golden. The poster was created by Joseph Christian Leyendecker in 1918 to get people to help in the World War I effort.

The United States entered World War I in 1917, three years after the conflict began. By November 1918, the war was over. During that time, the U.S. government sold war bonds to fund its participation in the war. The bonds were much like saving bonds, giving the government money now in exchange for more money later. Many of the posters that promoted war bonds were very patriotic. The poster on page 35 is a good example of such patriotism.

· ·

Directions | Use the poster on page 35 to answer the questions. Write complete sentences.

1. The woman in the poster is wearing a red, white, and blue robe. Does she look familiar? What does she represent?

   _____

   _____

2. What image is on the shield? What does that image represent?

   _____

   _____

3. The Boy Scout kneeling before the woman is offering her a sword with the Scout motto. What words are on the sword? Who or what should be prepared?

   _____

   _____

4. Is this poster effective? Would it make you help the war effort? Tell why or why not.

   _____

   _____

5. Do citizens have a duty or obligation to their nation in times of war? If so, what is that duty?

   _____

   _____

   _____

CONTINUED ▶

Buy Bonds, p. 2 ···

Posters often contain symbols. Who is this woman? What does she represent?

War bond poster, 1918

Posters often contain words. The words deliver the message of the poster.

Source: National Archives and Records Administration

Name _____   Date _____

What's So Funny? ....

A political cartoon is an illustration that contains a social or political message. Often a political cartoon tries to make you think a certain way about an issue. Political cartoons are not necessarily funny. Study the cartoon below. It was drawn by Charles Alston, an African American cartoonist, in 1943. **What is its message?**

The rifle suggests the man is a soldier.

The storm is a symbol. What does it represent?

Source: National Archives and Records Administration

I'm Going to See That You Grow Up in a Better World, Young Fellow

. . . .

Directions   **Use the cartoon to answer the questions. Write complete sentences. Use another sheet of paper.**

1. What does the storm represent?

2. Is the storm an effective symbol? Tell why or why not.

3. What is the main idea of this political cartoon?

4. Is the cartoon effective in persuading the reader? Explain.

The Black Death · 37 ·

In this unit, you will study documents on your own. Read or view each document carefully, and then answer the questions.

> **Remember, to understand a text document:**
>
> • Find out when, where, and by whom the document was created.
>
> • Find the purpose and main idea of the document.
>
> • Look up any unfamiliar words.

In the Middle Ages, a disease called the Black Death swept through Europe. The disease, also called the plague, killed over a third of Europe's population. In Great Britain, over two million people died of the plague.

It began in England in Dorsetshire . . . in the year of the Lord 1348, and immediately advancing from place to place it attacked men without warning and for the most part those who were healthy. Very many of those who were attacked in the morning it carried out of human affairs before noon. And no one whom it willed to die did it permit to live longer than three or four days. There was moreover no choice of persons, with the exception, at least, of a few rich people.

Anonymous

· ·

Directions First circle any unfamiliar words and look them up. Then write complete sentences to answer the questions.

1. Whom did the plague attack?

_____

_____

2. How long did people who got the plague live?

_____

_____

3. The report says that many who got the plague in the morning were "carried out of human affairs before noon." What does that statement mean?

_____

_____

_____

Name _____ Date _____

Great Charters ··

In 1215, English nobles forced King John to sign a list of rights and liberties called the Magna Carta. About 575 years later, some of the same rights and liberties appeared in the Bill of Rights in the Constitution of the United States.

(39) No free man shall be taken or imprisoned or stripped of his rights or possessions, or exiled or in any way destroyed, nor will we proceed with force against him, or send others to do so, except by the lawful judgment of his peers or by the law of the land.

from the Magna Carta, 1215

No person shall . . . be deprived of life, liberty, or property, without due process of law; nor shall private property be taken for public use, without just compensation.

from the Fifth Amendment to the Constitution of the United States, 1789

· ·

Directions | **Answer the questions. Write complete sentences. Use another sheet of paper if necessary.**

1. What are some unfamiliar words in the selections? Did you look them up in the dictionary? What do those words mean?

_____

_____

2. Due process means that people must be tried in courts if they are accused of a crime. Why is due process important?

_____

_____

3. How are the two selections similar? Are the rights given in the Fifth Amendment the same as the rights given in the Magna Carta? Explain.

_____

_____

_____

_____

_____

_____

Sir Isaac Newton ···

Sir Isaac Newton was a famous English scientist who lived from 1642 to 1727. He is best known for his experiment with gravity. As a young boy, he was keenly interested in how things worked.

Every one that knew Sir Isaac, or have heard of him, recount . . . his strange inventions, and extraordinary inclination for mechanics. That instead of playing among the other boys, when from school, he always busied himself making knick-knacks and models of wood in many kinds. . . . In particular they speak of his making a wooden clock. . . . About this time, a new windmill was set up near Grantham. . . . [Sir Isaac] became master enough to make a perfect model thereof. . . . but what was most extraordinary in its composition was that he put a mouse into it . . . and that the mouse made the mill turn round when he pleased.

Dr. Stukely, 1660

· ·

Directions Use the selection to answer the questions. Write complete sentences. Use another sheet of paper.

1. Circle any unfamiliar words. What do they mean?

2. What is an inclination?

3. What is a knick-knack?

4. How might Sir Isaac's boyhood experiences have made him a good scientist?

5. Do you think you could build a wooden clock? Tell why or why not.

Viva La France ·

After the American Revolution, people in other countries wished for freedom. In 1789, people in France started the French Revolution. Soon, they had overthrown the nobility that ran the country. A list of rights was issued. It became known as the Declaration of the Rights of Man and of the Citizen. It was approved by the National Assembly of France on August 26, 1789. Some of the rights are listed below.

1. Men are born and remain free and equal in rights. Social distinctions may be founded only upon the general good.

4. Liberty consists in the freedom to do everything which injures no one else; hence the exercise of the natural rights of each man has no limits except those which assure to the other members of the society the enjoyment of the same rights. These limits can only be determined by law.

6. Law is the expression of the general will. Every citizen has a right to participate personally, or through his representative, in its foundation. It must be the same for all, whether it protects or punishes.

7. No person shall be accused, arrested, or imprisoned except in the cases and according to the forms prescribed by law. . . .

10. No one shall be disquieted on account of his opinions, including his religious views, provided their manifestation does not disturb the public order established by law.

from the Declaration of the Rights of Man and of the Citizen, 1789

· ·

Directions | Use the listed rights to answer the questions. Write complete sentences. Use another sheet of paper.

1. Which of the rights listed deals with freedom of speech?

2. According to the list of rights, what is "law"?

3. According to the list of rights, what is "liberty"? At what point does liberty end?

4. Review the rights discussed on page 38. Which of the rights above is similar to the rights discussed on page 38?

Name _____ Date _____

A Time of Change ··

On January 20, 1965, Lyndon B. Johnson became the new President of the United States. At that time, the world was in turmoil. The Cold War caused great tension between nations, and the war in Vietnam was expanding. The Space Race was in full swing, and civil rights was a controversial topic. In the midst of all those events, Johnson delivered a stirring inaugural speech.

Lyndon B. Johnson being sworn in as president

My fellow countrymen:

On this occasion the oath I have taken before you and before God is not mine alone, but ours together. We are one nation and one people. Our fate as a nation and our future as a people rest not upon one citizen but upon all citizens. . . .

For every generation there is a destiny. For some, history decides. For this generation, the choice must be our own.

Even now, a rocket moves toward Mars. It reminds us that the world will not be the same for our children, or even for ourselves in a short span of years. . . .

Ours is a time of change—rapid and fantastic change—bearing the secrets of nature, multiplying the nations, placing in uncertain hands new weapons for mastery and destruction, shaking old values and uprooting old ways.

from Lyndon B. Johnson's inaugural address, January 20, 1965

· ·

Directions Use Johnson's speech to answer the questions. Write complete sentences. Use another sheet of paper.

1. Does this portion of Johnson's speech sound optimistic or fearful? What words or ideas suggest this feeling? Explain.

2. In the third sentence, Johnson speaks of the fate of the nation. He says that the fate and future of the nation "rest not upon one citizen but upon all citizens." What does he mean?

3. Is the world still in a time of "rapid and fantastic change"? Give some examples.

4. If you were elected president and had to give an inaugural speech, what would you say? Write a few lines of your speech.

Name _____   Date _____

Life Span ···

People around the world have different life expectancies. That term means how long they will live. The chart below shows some of these average life spans. Remember, charts provide much information in a small space. They make it easy to compare information. Charts help you learn facts quickly.

> **Remember, to get the most from a chart:**
> • Read the title to learn what the chart is about.
> • Read the column headings to learn what information is included.
> • Read all the information in the rows.

Life Expectancy at Birth, 1999

Country	Male	Female
United States	73	80
Brazil	59	69
Sweden	77	82
Japan	77	83
Egypt	60	64

Source: The CIA World Fact Book

· ·

Directions   Use the chart to answer the questions.

1. In which country does a man have the shortest life expectancy?

_____

2. In which country does a woman have the longest life expectancy?

_____

3. What conclusion can you draw from the chart?

_____

_____

4. Find each country on the chart on a map. Where are they located? Could climate affect life expectancy? Explain on another sheet of paper.

Chinese Conflicts ·

A chart organizes information in a compact way. The chart below shows wars involving the nation of China. Various nations have tried to take over China. Each time China has resisted that takeover.

China: Wars of Resistance

1839–1842	Anglo-Chinese (Opium) War
1856–1860	Anglo-French War
1894–1895	Sino-Japanese War
1898–1900	Boxer Rebellion (against the British)
1911–1912	Rebellion and the End of the Chinese Monarchy

· ·

Directions   **Use the chart to answer the questions.**

1. Which of the wars in the chart lasted the longest?

_____

2. Which war ended in 1900?

_____

3. In what year did the Chinese monarchy end?

_____

4. The chart shows that the Chinese were involved in many wars of resistance. Do you think the Chinese were successful in the wars? Explain why.

_____

_____

_____

_____

_____

_____

_____

Ancient Egypt ·

A chart can show the effects of an event. Study the chart below. It shows some of the rulers of ancient Egypt and their accomplishments. Dates B.C. get bigger the farther back in history you go. For example, 1500 B.C. came before 1400 B.C.

Some Rulers of Egypt's New Kingdom, 1546–1237 B.C.

Name/Reign	Accomplishments
Amenhotep I (1546–1526 B.C.)	He began building an Egyptian empire by attacking neighboring countries.
Hatshepsut (1503–1482 B.C.)	She seized power from her stepson and ruled as a pharaoh.
Akhenaten (1379–1362 B.C.)	He replaced traditional state religion with a monotheistic religion based on belief in one god.
Tutankhamen (1361–1352 B.C.)	He began returning Egypt to the traditional state religion but died young.
Ramses II (1304–1237 B.C.)	He made peace with Egypt's enemies, the Hittites, and started a massive building program.

· ·

Directions Use the chart to answer the questions. Write complete sentences.

1. Which of these rulers was the most recent in history?

_____

2. Which of these rulers was the most warlike? Why?

_____

3. In what main way was Hatshepsut different from the other rulers in the chart?

_____

4. What was the accomplishment of Ramses II?

_____

_____

Name _____ Date _____

Independence in Latin America ·

A time line shows the order of events in a certain period of time. The events and time they happen are presented along a vertical or horizontal line. This line shows the sequence of events. The time line below shows when countries in Latin America gained their independence.

> **Remember, to get the most from a time line:**
> • Read the title of the time line carefully.
> • Read all the labels in the time line.
> • Read the times or years in the time line.
> • Use your finger to follow the movement of the time line.

Latin American Independence

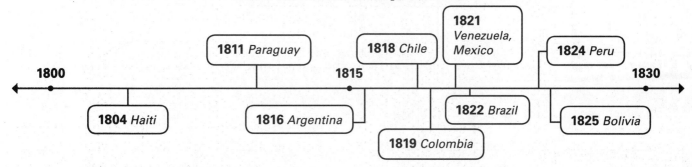

· ·

Directions Use the time line to answer the questions. Darken the circle by the best answer for each question.

1. Which was the first Latin American country to gain independence?
   Ⓐ Peru   Ⓒ Haiti
   Ⓑ Bolivia   Ⓓ Chile

2. Which Latin American country gained independence in 1819?
   Ⓐ Argentina   Ⓒ Chile
   Ⓑ Colombia   Ⓓ Brazil

3. In which year did Mexico and Venezuela gain independence?
   Ⓐ 1821   Ⓒ 1824
   Ⓑ 1822   Ⓓ 1825

4. Which was the last Latin American country to gain independence?
   Ⓐ Haiti   Ⓒ Brazil
   Ⓑ Bolivia   Ⓓ Peru

· ·

Directions Answer the question on another sheet of paper. Write complete sentences.

5. Using the evidence on the time line, what conclusion can you make about Latin American independence?

Name _____ Date _____

World War II ··

World War II began in 1939 when Germany invaded Poland. The time line below shows events in that conflict.

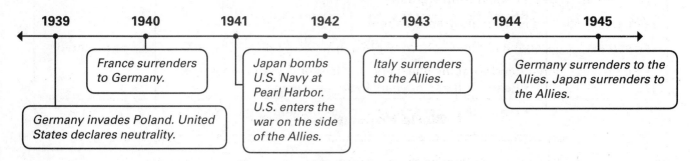

World War II

| 1939 | 1940 | 1941 | 1942 | 1943 | 1944 | 1945 |

France surrenders to Germany.

Germany invades Poland. United States declares neutrality.

Japan bombs U.S. Navy at Pearl Harbor. U.S. enters the war on the side of the Allies.

Italy surrenders to the Allies.

Germany surrenders to the Allies. Japan surrenders to the Allies.

···

Directions Use the time line to answer the questions. Write complete sentences.

1. In which year did Italy surrender to the Allies?

_____

2. In which year did France surrender to Germany?

_____

3. When World War II started in 1939, the United States declared neutrality. What does *neutrality* mean?

_____

_____

4. What event caused the United States to enter World War II?

_____

_____

5. What two events signaled the end of World War II in 1945?

_____

_____

Name _____ Date _____

World Population ·

The number of people in the world continues to grow. The bar graph below shows world population growth throughout history.

> **Remember, to get the most from a graph:**
> • Read the title to see what the graph is about.
> • Read the labels on the left and bottom of the graph to see what information is being presented.
> • Be sure you understand what the line, bars, or slices on a graph represent.

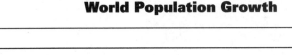

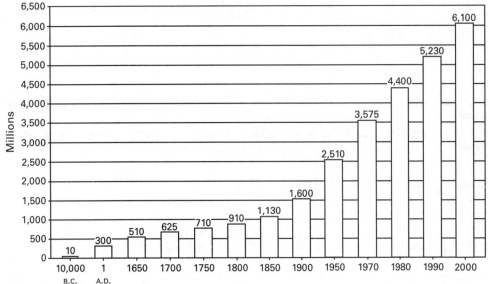

· ·

Directions   Use the bar graph to answer the questions. Write complete sentences.

1. Look at the numbers on top of the bars. The number above 1850—1,130—means 1 billion, 130 million people. How many people were in the world in 1900?

_____

2. How many people were in the world in 1 A.D.?

_____

3. Is the world population increasing or decreasing?

_____

4. Would you say population growth after 1900 was faster or slower than growth before 1900? Explain.

_____

Name _____ Date _____

Power Up ·

A pie graph or circle graph uses wedge-shaped "slices" to compare a part to the whole. The **whole is always 100%.** The pie graph below tells about energy sources that fuel the world's needs.

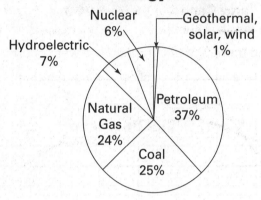

World Energy Sources

· ·

Directions | Use the graph to answer the questions. Write complete sentences.

1. What is the main energy source for the world's needs?

_____

2. From which energy source does the world get 25% of its needs met?

_____

3. What percentage of the world's energy needs are filled by nuclear power?

_____

4. From which sources does the world get the least energy?

_____

5. As the graph shows, the world gets most of its energy needs met from fossil fuels (petroleum, coal, natural gas). Do you think the world will have enough energy for its needs if fossil fuels run out? Explain using evidence from the graph.

_____

_____

_____

_____

Name _____ Date _____

Get a Job! ....

A double-line graph has two lines that show change. Each line represents something different. The double-line graph below shows unemployment in the United States and Canada from 1970 to 2000.

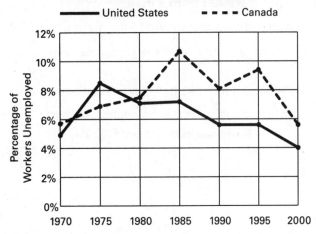

Unemployment Rates in the United States and Canada, 1970–2000

——— United States - - - - Canada

Directions / **Use the graph to answer the questions. Write complete sentences.**

1. In 1975, which country had a higher rate of unemployment?

_____

2. In 1985, which country had a higher rate of unemployment?

_____

3. From 1990 to 1995, did unemployment in Canada increase or decrease?

_____

4. From 1990 to 1995, what did the unemployment rate in the United States do?

_____

5. What conclusion can you draw about unemployment in the two countries during this time period? Use evidence from the graph to explain.

_____

_____

_____

_____

Name _____ Date _____

European Colonies in the Americas ·····························

Maps can tell many kinds of information. They can tell about a place at a certain time in history. The map below shows three different nations that had colonies in the Western Hemisphere in 1784—Great Britain, Spain, and Portugal.

> **Remember, to get the most from a map:**
>
> • Read the title of the map to see what information the map presents.
>
> • Find the map legend or key. It tells what patterns or symbols on the map mean.
>
> • Find the distance scale. It tells how far apart places are.

Colonization as of 1784

Directions   Use the map to answer the questions. Write complete sentences.

1. Which country had the greatest area of colonization in North America and Central America?

_____

_____

2. Which country had the greatest area of colonization in eastern South America?

_____

_____

3. About how far is the southern tip of South America from the Equator?

_____

_____

African Colonies ·

Maps can tell many kinds of information. They can tell about a place at a certain time in history. The map below shows the different nations that had colonies in Africa.

Colonialism in Africa in the Early 1900s

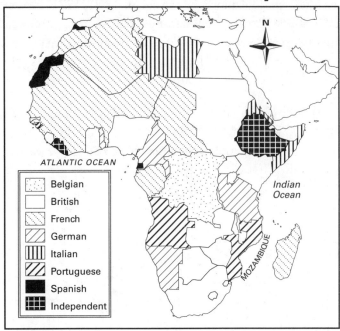

· ·

Directions / **Darken the circle by the best answer for each question.**

1. Which of the following colonial powers had a colony with no seaport?

    Ⓐ Belgium

    Ⓑ Italy

    Ⓒ Britain

    Ⓓ France

2. Although Portugal had been a colonial power in Africa since the fifteenth century, corruption and poor management reduced Portugal's holdings to Angola and Mozambique, both of which became free in 1975. Which was the <u>most likely</u> reason for Portugal's decline in Africa?

    Ⓐ civil war at home

    Ⓑ economic depression abroad

    Ⓒ crop failure in the colonies

    Ⓓ inefficiency in colonial matters

3. Which of the following statements is supported by the map?

    Ⓐ Germany did not establish territories in Africa.

    Ⓑ Portugal established colonial territories mainly in north Africa.

    Ⓒ Britain and France annexed the majority of African territory.

    Ⓓ Spain annexed more African territory than Portugal.

4. Which of the following is a conclusion supported by the information?

    Ⓐ Colonialism thrived in the twentieth century.

    Ⓑ Africa escaped most colonialism.

    Ⓒ Without World War II, Africa would still be colonized.

    Ⓓ The Congo suffered the most.

Marco Polo ··

Sometimes maps are used to illustrate text. Notice how the map on this page gives more information about the topic. Maps can also show routes.

Marco Polo became a world explorer at the age of 17. In 1271, he set out for China with his father and uncle, who were Venetian merchants. After three years of travel across central Asia by ship and camels, the Polos arrived in Shang-tu at the summer palace of Kublai Khan, the Mongol emperor of China. Marco quickly became a favorite of the khan and for 17 years traveled in China as his representative.

Near the end of this time, the Polos were ready to return home. At first the khan was unwilling to let them leave. But in 1292 he agreed and allowed them to sail to Persia. From there they were able to reach Venice in 1295—24 years after they left it.

The Travels of Marco Polo

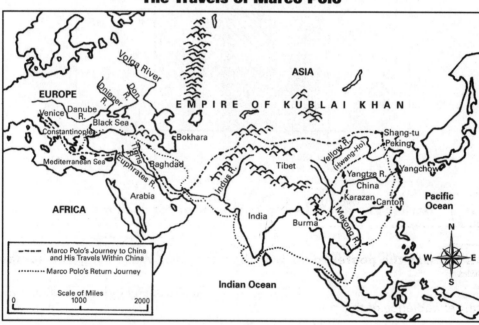

| Directions | Use the map and the text to answer the questions. Write complete sentences. Use another sheet of paper. |

1. From which European city did the Polos leave in 1271?

2. About how far is Venice from Shang-tu?

3. Did Marco Polo return straight to Venice when he left China? Explain using evidence from the map.

Name _____ Date _____

Warning! ··

Posters try to influence people. They try to make people do or not do something. Often posters will contain bold type and images. Look at the poster on this page. It was used as a workplace safety poster during World War I. It urges people to use care in their work. The poster was created by L. N. Britton in 1917.

> **Remember, to get the most from a poster:**
>
> • Study the poster. To which words or images are your eyes drawn?
>
> • How is the main idea portrayed in the poster? What influences the viewer?
>
> • Think about the audience. Who would be influenced by this poster?

Source: National Archives and Records Administration

World War I safety poster, 1917–1918

··

Directions Use the poster to answer the questions. Write complete sentences.

1. Who is the target audience of this poster?

_____

2. What words on the poster are emphasized? What effect do they have?

_____

_____

3. What is the main idea of this poster?

_____

_____

4. What might happen if a person is careless in the workplace?

_____

The North Pole ···

Robert E. Peary was a driven explorer. He wanted to be the first person to reach the North Pole. On April 6, 1909, Peary claimed, he and his party reached the North Pole—the first people to reach the North Pole. The photograph shows Peary's sledge party at the North Pole. Peary is not in the picture. At the center is Matthew Henson, Peary's longtime associate.

Source: National Archives and Records Administration

North Pole, April 7, 1909

· ·

Directions Use the photograph to answer the questions. Write complete sentences.

1. When and where was this photograph taken?

_____

2. Is this a photograph of an important event? Tell why or why not.

_____

_____

_____

_____

_____

Name _____ Date _____

Matthew Henson ···

Some cartoons are educational. They give you information about people in history. The cartoon on this page is about Arctic explorer Matthew Henson. It was drawn in 1943 by Charles Alston. Compare this cartoon to the photograph on page 54.

Source: National Archives and Records Administration

· ·

Directions   **Use the cartoon to answer the questions. Write complete sentences. Use another sheet of paper.**

1. According to the cartoon, was Robert Peary the first man to reach the North Pole? Explain.

2. Does this cartoon make the photograph on page 54 more interesting or informative? Explain using evidence from the photograph and the cartoon.

Wasting Resources ···

A political cartoon contains a social or political message. A political cartoon tries to make a reader think a certain way about an issue. The political cartoon below illustrates a common problem today. But it was drawn in 1943 by Charles Alston. What is its message?

> **Remember, to get the most from a political cartoon:**
>
> • Study the images and words in the cartoon. Important labels are often included.
>
> • Symbols are often used in political cartoons. Try to figure out what the symbols mean.
>
> • Some cartoons have captions or voice bubbles. Do you believe what is being said?

Source: National Archives and Records Administration

··

Directions | Use the political cartoon to answer the questions. **Write complete sentences. Use another sheet of paper.**

1. What does the lake behind the dam represent?

2. What does the leak in the dam represent?

3. What is the main idea of this political cartoon? Is the cartoon effective in presenting that main idea?

Remember the *Maine*! ···

On February 15, 1898, the U.S. battleship *Maine* mysteriously exploded. It quickly sank to the bottom of the harbor at Havana, Cuba, taking with it 266 U.S. sailors. Though the explosion was later determined to be accidental, many at the time blamed the Spanish government in Cuba. The Spanish-American War began two months later.

Source: National Archives and Records Administration

Torn Loose, April 17, 1898

···

Directions   **Use the political cartoon to answer the questions. Write complete sentences. Use another sheet of paper.**

1. Who does the man in the cartoon represent?

2. Describe the action in the cartoon.

3. Why is the man in a warlike mood?

4. The hand representing peace was holding the man's coattails, but he has torn loose. What is the main idea of this cartoon?

The Korean War ···

You may be asked to study several documents about a topic. Then you may need to answer questions or write an essay about the documents. The rest of this unit will give you practice in this process.

War started on the Korean peninsula in 1950 when North Korea invaded South Korea. The time line below tells about events in that conflict.

The Korean War

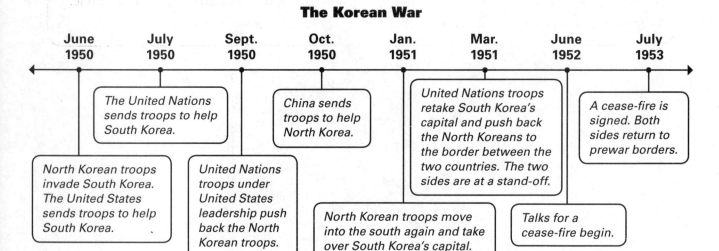

···

Directions | Use the time line to answer the questions. Write complete sentences.

1. What event started the Korean War?

_____

_____

2. Who fought on each side in the Korean War?

_____

_____

3. What is a cease-fire? When was a cease-fire signed?

_____

_____

CONTINUED ▶

58

The Korean War, p. 2 ···

> **To do your best with several documents:**
>
> • Study each document carefully.
>
> • Read all titles and labels, and study all images.
>
> • Think about how the documents fit together and the information they present about the topic.
>
> • Think about all the documents as you answer the questions or write the essay.

The map below gives details about the first few months of the Korean War.

· ·

Directions   **Use the map to answer the questions. Write complete sentences.**

1. What was the prewar boundary between North Korea and South Korea?

_____

2. During the first few months of the war, which side seemed to be winning? Use evidence from the map to explain.

_____

_____

3. During the fall of 1950, which side seemed to be winning? Use evidence from the map to explain.

_____

_____

Modern Mexico ··

After Mexico became independent, different groups fought for control of the government. In its first 55 years, Mexico had 75 leaders. In 1876, Porfirio Diaz took over the Mexican government. At the time, Mexico's economy was in shambles. Foreign investors would not risk their money in a nation without strong leadership. Diaz wanted to show them that Mexico had a firm leader in charge.

Investors did begin spending on Mexico's economy. Foreign capital—money spent for production or investment—was put to immediate use. It bought modern equipment. It also paid for developing Mexico's natural resources. An American investor bought land and explored for oil. As a result, Mexico became one of the world's largest oil suppliers by the early 1900s.

The chart below shows the growth in Mexico's gross national product. The gross national product is the total value of everything a nation produces. A country's gross national product indicates the growth and health of its economy.

Mexico's Economic Growth Indicators
Gross National Product*

Year	Mining	Agriculture	Manufacturing	Oil	Transportation	Other Activities	Total
1895	431	2,107	806	none	204	5,315	8,863
1900	541	1,991	1,232	none	237	5,890	9,891
1905	848	2,543	1,475	1	299	7,294	12,460
1910	1,022	2,692	1,663	19	295	7,833	13,524

*in millions of pesos at 1950 prices

· ·

Directions Use the chart to answer the questions.

1. How much money did Mexico make from oil in 1895? _____

2. From 1895 to 1910, did Mexico's gross national product get larger or smaller? _____

3. Would you say Mexico's economy improved or worsened during the years shown?

_____

_____

_____

_____

_____

_____

CONTINUED ▶

Modern Mexico, p. 2 ··

In 1904, the United States government published a book about the land and economy of Mexico. A short excerpt from the book follows.

> The financial question in Mexico has been one of the most perplexing problems that ever presented itself to the statesman's mind. From the moment the country emerged from its centuries of colonial rule it was confronted with the gravest economic difficulties. . . . Without any previous experience, they were compelled to change, improvise, and try new systems. The many revolutions and consequent changes in adminstrations served but to add to the perplexity of the situation, and it has required a high order of ability to bring the finances of the country to their present condition.
>
> from *Mexico: Geographical Sketch, Natural Resources Laws . . .*, 1904

· ·

Directions / Use the chart and text to answer the questions. Write complete sentences.

1. What does the reading selection say happened to Mexico after it emerged from foreign rule?

_____

_____

2. According to the selection, why was the Mexican economy in poor shape?

_____

_____

3. Do the chart and selection suggest that Mexico's economy was improving? Provide evidence to support your answer.

_____

_____

_____

_____

_____

_____

_____

CONTINUED ▶

Name _____ Date _____

Modern Mexico, p. 3 ···

The bar graph below shows how much foreign capital was invested in Mexico.

Foreign Capital in Mexican Mining and Industry, 1896–1907

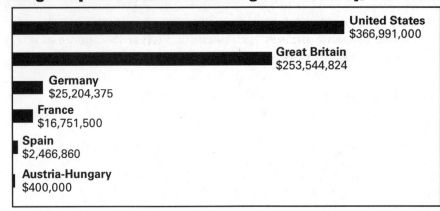

United States
$366,991,000

Great Britain
$253,544,824

Germany
$25,204,375

France
$16,751,500

Spain
$2,466,860

Austria-Hungary
$400,000

· ·

Directions Use the graph, chart, and reading selection to answer the questions.
Write complete sentences.

1. Which foreign nation invested the most money in the Mexican economy?

_____

2. Using evidence from the three documents, give reasons the Mexican economy improved.

_____

_____

_____

3. Which of these three documents is most effective in telling about the history of the Mexican economy? Give reasons for your choice.

_____

_____

_____

_____

_____

_____

_____

Practice Test ·······································

You will probably have to take tests about historical documents. Learn how using this practice test. Study each document carefully. You will be using them to write an essay at the end of the test.

Directions | **This practice test is based on documents 1 through 4. It will test your ability to work with historical documents. In Part A, look at each document and answer the questions after it. Use your answers to the questions in Part A to help you write your essay in Part B.**

Historical Background

> Christopher Columbus believed the world was round. He believed he could sail west to get east, in his case, the East Indies, or India. He didn't know there was a rather large land mass between Europe and India. Columbus sailed with 90 men on three ships, leaving Spain on August 3, 1492. The ships covered about 4,000 miles. On October 12, 1492, a sailor sighted land. Thinking he was near India, Columbus called the place the West Indies, and he claimed it for Spain.

· ·

Directions | **For Part A, study EACH document carefully and answer the questions after it. These answers will help you write your essay.**

For Part B, use the information from the documents, your answers from Part A, and your knowledge of social studies to write a well-organized essay. The focus of your essay will be the voyages of Christopher Columbus.

Source: Library of Congress

First sight of the New World

GO ON ▶

Name _____ Date _____

Part A: Short-Answer Questions ·······························

 **The following documents show information about the voyages of Christopher Columbus. Study each document carefully. Then answer the questions that follow it in the space provided.**

In August 1492, Columbus left Spain with three ships: the Niña, the Pinta, and the Santa Maria. After two months, the voyagers spotted land in the Bahamas, thinking they were near India.

📜 **Document 1**

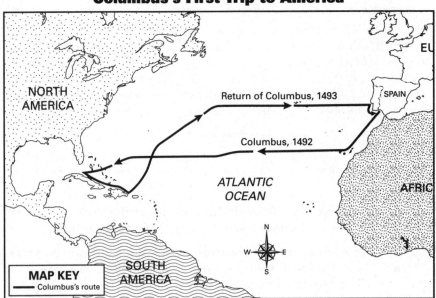

Columbus's First Trip to America

···

Directions **Use the map to answer the questions. Write complete sentences.**

1. Did Columbus and his ships immediately sail west from Spain? Use evidence from the map to answer.

_____

_____

2. Did Columbus and his ships ever reach the mainland of the United States? Use evidence from the map to answer.

_____

_____

3. When did Columbus return to Spain after his first voyage?

_____

_____

GO ON ▶

Name _____ Date _____

Columbus kept a journal during his voyage. In the excerpt below, he tells of the first sight of land and the first trip ashore in the New World. Believing he had indeed reached land near India, he called the people there Indians.

Document 2

The land appeared two hours after midnight, about two leagues away. We furled all sail except the *treo*, the mainsail with no bonnets, and we jogged off and on until Friday morning, when we came to an island. We saw naked people, and I went ashore in a boat with armed men. . . .

When we stepped ashore we saw fine green trees, streams everywhere and different kinds of fruit. I called to the two captains to jump ashore with the rest, asking them to bear solemn witness that in the presence of them all I was taking possession of this island for their Lord and Lady the King and Queen. . . .

Soon many of the islanders gathered round us. . . . I gave some of them red bonnets and glass beads which they hung round their necks, and many other things of small value, at which they were so delighted and so eager to please us that we could not believe it. . . . They took anything, and gave willingly whatever they had.

from *The Journal of Christopher Columbus*, October 12, 1492

. . . .

Directions Use the journal entry to answer the questions. Write complete sentences.

1. On what date was land first sighted by Columbus and his men? _____
_____

2. On what day did Columbus first step ashore in the New World? _____
_____

3. How does Columbus describe the island and the people he met there? _____
_____
_____
_____
_____
_____
_____
_____

GO ON ▶

Name_____ Date_____

The illustration below shows Columbus claiming the New World for Spain.

 Document 3

Source: Library of Congress

Columbus lands in the New World.

- -

Directions **Use the illustration to answer the questions. Write complete sentences.**

1. How do you think Columbus and his men felt when they stepped ashore in the New World?

_____

_____

2. Does the illustration help to make Columbus's journal entry on page 65 easier to understand? Explain using evidence from the journal entry and the illustration.

_____

_____

_____

_____

_____

GO ON ▶

Name _____ Date _____

Columbus made four voyages to the New World. The time line below gives details about his voyages.

Document 4

Christopher Columbus Time Line

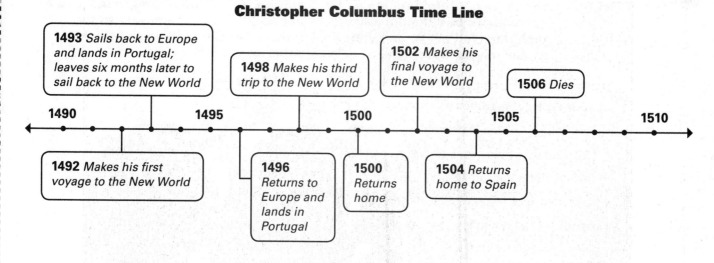

1493 *Sails back to Europe and lands in Portugal; leaves six months later to sail back to the New World*

1498 *Makes his third trip to the New World*

1502 *Makes his final voyage to the New World*

1506 *Dies*

1490 1495 1500 1505 1510

1492 *Makes his first voyage to the New World*

1496 *Returns to Europe and lands in Portugal*

1500 *Returns home*

1504 *Returns home to Spain*

Directions Use the time line to answer the questions.

1. When did Columbus make his second voyage to the New World?

_____

2. When did Columbus make his third voyage to the New World?

_____

3. When did Columbus make his final voyage to the New World?

_____

4. When did Columbus die?

_____

5. Why do you think Columbus kept returning to the New World?

_____

_____

_____

_____

_____

_____

GO ON ▶

Unit 3: Listening on Your Own
Voices: World History, SV 9781419036392

Part B: Essay ································

Directions | Write a well-developed essay about Christopher Columbus and his voyages to the New World. Include an introduction, supporting paragraphs, and a conclusion. Use the documents on pages 64–67, your answers to the questions in Part A, and your knowledge of social studies to help you organize your ideas. Use your own paper to write the essay.

In your essay, remember to discuss:

• why Columbus decided to sail west across the Atlantic Ocean

• the route Columbus took to reach the New World

• his description of the New World and its inhabitants

• his claiming of the New World for Spain

• his other voyages to the New World

After you complete your essay, look at the following list and check your writing. Go back and make any corrections to your essay that might be needed.

• Did you remember to answer ALL parts of the question in your essay?

• Did you use as many documents as you could in your essay?

• Did you include information you already knew about the topic?

• Did you express yourself clearly?

• Did you stay on the topic and not add any unnecessary information?

• Did you write an introduction that explains what your essay is about?

• Did you write a conclusion that sums up what you wrote about in your essay?

After you have revised your essay, compare it to the sample essay on page 69.

GO ON ▶

Sample Essay ···

The following essay answers all of the parts of the writing task and uses the documents and some outside information. It develops ideas well, has good organization, and expresses ideas clearly. It would receive a good score. Compare this sample essay to your essay about Christopher Columbus.

Christopher Columbus believed that the world was round. He believed he could get to Asia by sailing west across the Atlantic Ocean. Perhaps doubtful of his own beliefs, after leaving Spain, Columbus and his three ships sailed along the coast of Africa. Finally, the voyage turned west. After two months of sailing, Columbus and his crew sighted some of the islands in the Caribbean Sea. Columbus's route is shown in Document 1.

On October 12, 1492, land was sighted shortly after midnight. The ships sailed back and forth until dawn. Then Columbus and a group of men landed on an island and claimed it for Spain. Columbus described the island as covered with trees, with many kinds of fruit and streams cutting across the land. The islanders were friendly, and Columbus gave them colorful trinkets. The islanders would take anything they were offered, and they freely shared what they had. Columbus makes these observations in his journal entry in Document 2.

The illustration in Document 3 shows Columbus claiming the New World for Spain, which had funded his voyage. Columbus thought he had landed on islands near India, so he called the people on the island Indians. Columbus and his men must have been relieved and grateful to reach land after so long at sea. Their weapons suggest they might have expected to meet hostile people.

Columbus returned to Europe and landed in Portugal in 1493. Six months later, he again sailed to the New World and explored more of the islands of the Caribbean. Over the next nine years, Columbus made two more voyages to the New World, one in 1498 and his last voyage in 1502. Each time he explored more of the area he had first visited in 1492. He returned home for the last time in 1504. Two years later, Columbus died in Spain. The time line in Document 4 clearly shows the major events in Columbus's life as an explorer.

Practice Test 1 ·

Directions This practice test is based on documents 1 through 8. It will test your ability to work with historical documents. In Part A, look at each document and answer the questions after it. Consider the context and point of view of each document. Use your answers to the questions in Part A to help you write your essay in Part B.

Historical Background

Egypt was one of the first areas of civilization. Egypt has been called "the gift of the Nile." Without the Nile River, all of Egypt would be a desert. Around 5000 B.C., communities began to form along the Nile. These early Egyptians developed a system of writing and a form of government. They worshiped many gods and believed in an afterlife. They were also great builders. The Great Pyramid in Giza was built around 2500 B.C. This structure still stands today, over 4,500 years later.

· ·

Directions For **Part A**, study EACH document carefully and answer the questions after it. These answers will help you write your essay.

For **Part B**, use the information from the documents, your answers from Part A, and your knowledge of social studies to write a well-organized essay. The focus of your essay will be about ancient Egypt.

Source: Metropolitan Museum of Art

The mummy mask of King Tutankhamen

Name _____ Date _____

Part A: Short-Answer Questions ·····························

 Directions The following documents show information about ancient Egypt. Study each document carefully. Then answer the questions that follow it.

The map below shows some of the cities in ancient Egypt.

📜 Document 1

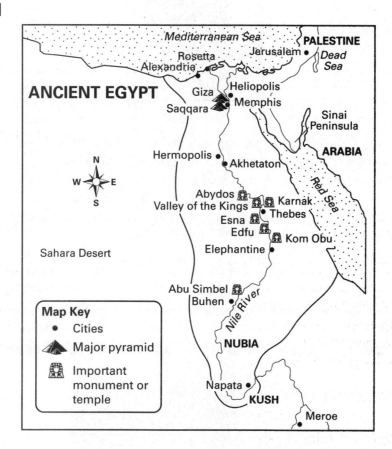

Directions Use the map to answer the questions. Write complete sentences.

1. Which part of Egypt has most of the major pyramids? _____

2. Near which valley are many temples and monuments? _____

_____

3. Which desert covers most of Egypt? _____

4. What body of water lies to the east of Egypt? _____

5. What body of water lies to the north of Egypt? _____

GO ON ▶

The ancient Egyptians were one of the first groups to develop a writing system. Their system is now known as hieroglyphics. This word comes from Greek words that mean "sacred writings." The Egyptians also made a kind of paper called papyrus.

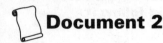 Document 2

The Egyptians made ink by mixing soot and vegetable gum with water. With this they wrote on the papyrus by means of a pointed reed. A book was a roll of written papyrus, and a reader had to hold it with both hands, unrolling it with one hand at one end while rolling it up with the other hand at the other end as he read. A papyrus book was kept packed in a jar. A library consisted of a number of shelves of papyrus jars, each labeled to show the subject treated.

from *Modern Times and the Living Past*, by Henry W. Elson, 1921

∙ ∙

Directions   **Use the text excerpt to answer the questions. Write complete sentences.**

1. How did the Egyptians make ink?

_____

_____

2. How did a person read a papyrus book?

_____

_____

3. What if libraries today were like the ones in ancient Egypt? Would books be easy to read?

_____

_____

_____

_____

_____

GO ON ▶

The ancient Egyptians had many gods and goddesses. Animals were important to the Egyptians, too. Many of the gods and goddesses had animal features. The phoenix represented the Egyptians' belief in an afterlife and suggests a reason for mummies.

Document 3

In every part of Egypt two great gods, Isis and Osiris, were worshiped. Isis is the wife of Osiris. Ra the sun-god was the greatest of the gods; he was supposed to be the representative of the Supreme Being. And yet Osiris was the most popular god. Ra was generally represented as a hawk-headed man, and usually with a solar disk upon his head. . . .

At Heliopolis were kept two animals sacred to Ra, the black bull and the phoenix. The phoenix was a bird which the Egyptians regarded as the emblem of immortality; a bird which never died, but when it was burned, sprang up again, full-grown, from its ashes, ready to renew its activities.

The Egyptians held it as a central feature of their faith, that "man was not made to die," that we were to live a future life, that death does not end all. . . . The greatest event in a man's life happened after his death.

from *Gods and Devils of Mankind*, by Frank Dobbins, Samuel Williams, and Isaac Hall, 1897

Directions Use the text excerpt to answer the questions. Write complete sentences.

1. Which of the Egyptian gods was regarded as the greatest?

_____

2. How does the story of the phoenix symbolize the Egyptians' belief in life after death?

_____

_____

_____

_____

_____

_____

_____

_____

_____

GO ON ▶

The ancient Egyptians also worshiped cats. The goddess Pasht was the daughter of Osiris and Isis. She was the goddess of cats, the rising sun, the moon, and good harvests. Pasht, who was known by many names, was often pictured with the head of a cat and the body of a young woman. The Egyptians believed that by worshiping cats, they were also worshiping Pasht.

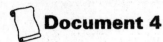 **Document 4**

Source: *Gods and Devils of Mankind, 1897*

Pasht, the cat-headed goddess

. . . .

Directions   Use the illustration and the text on page 73 to answer the questions. Write complete sentences.

1. Who were the parents of Pasht?

_____

2. Describe Pasht's appearance.

_____

_____

3. Why do you think the Egyptians worshiped cats?

_____

_____

GO ON ▶

Near Giza in Egypt are several pyramids. The three largest pyramids are the tombs of the pharaohs Cheops, Chephren, and Mycerinus. Near the Great Pyramid of Cheops is the mysterious Sphinx, a lion with the head of a man.

Document 5

The largest of these is the pyramid of Cheops. This is 480 feet high, and contains more than ten million . . . cubic yards of stone. The pyramid is so placed that its four sides exactly face the four points of the compass. . . . At the foot of the pyramids is the great Sphinx. This is a monument of a man-headed lion, nearly ninety feet long and seventy-four feet high. Its face is twenty-six feet long. It is carved out of solid rock. This great Sphinx is said to be the image of the god Har-ma-chu, the setting sun.

from *Gods and Devils of Mankind*, by Frank Dobbins, Samuel Williams, and Isaac Hall, 1897

. . . .

Directions **Use the text excerpt to answer the questions. Write complete sentences.**

1. How tall is the Great Pyramid of Cheops?

_____

2. What is unusual about the placement of the Great Pyramid of Cheops?

_____

_____

3. Describe the Sphinx.

_____

_____

_____

_____

_____

_____

_____

_____

GO ON ▶

Name _____ Date _____

The photograph below shows the Great Pyramid and the Sphinx near Giza.

Document 6

Source: Corbis Royalty Free

The Great Pyramid and the Sphinx, Giza, Egypt

. . . .

Directions | Use the photograph and the text on page 75 to answer the questions. Write complete sentences.

1. The Sphinx is thousands of years old. Based on the photograph, how do you think time has affected the Sphinx?

_____

_____

2. Does the photograph make the description on page 75 easier to understand? Explain.

_____

_____

_____

3. Why do you think the Egyptians built these huge pyramids and statues? Explain.

_____

_____

_____

GO ON ▶

Name _____ Date _____

The pyramids were used as tombs for the Egyptian pharaohs and their relatives. Usually the tombs were filled with objects the dead would need in the afterlife. These objects ranged from food and clothes to priceless jewels. Many of the pyramids were looted by tomb robbers. Other tombs were discovered by archaeologists. The treasures from these are on display in museums around the world.

Document 7

The most important discovery in the history of Egyptian excavations was that of the tomb of Tutankhamen (toot-ahnk-ah´-men), a pharaoh who lived nearly 1400 years B.C. Near the site of ancient Thebes, the important discovery was made in November 1922 by an English excavator named Howard Carter, assisted by Lord Carnarvon. . . . The treasures in this tomb were astonishing in their splendor, being well preserved in the dry Egyptian climate. The treasure chamber is reached by a passage through solid rock.

Among the treasures discovered in the tomb of Tutankhamen are the throne, gem-studded chariots, alabaster vases, boxes of mummified meats as food for the king in his passage to the next world; also an enormous amount of furniture, jewels of gold, precious stones innumerable, and ornaments of many varieties.

from *Modern Times and the Living Past*, by Henry W. Elson, 1921

. . . .

Directions   **Use the text excerpt to answer the questions. Write complete sentences.**

1. Who discovered the tomb of King Tutankhamen?

   _____

2. What were some of the treasures found in the tomb?

   _____

   _____

3. Why do you think the Egyptians placed all these treasures in the tombs of their dead pharaohs?

   _____

   _____

   _____

   _____

   _____

   _____

GO ON ▶

Name _____ Date _____

Howard Carter was one of the most famous archaeologists working in Egypt. He began his work as an artist sketching relics at excavations. In 1899, when he was only 25, he became responsible for supervising archaeology along the Nile Valley. In 1908, Carter met Lord Carnarvon and became supervisor of excavations that Carnarvon funded. In 1922, Carter discovered the tomb of the young pharaoh, Tutankhamen. It turned out to be one of the major archaeological finds in history.

 Document 8

Source: Ashmolean Museum, Oxford, England

Howard Carter and Lord Carnarvon at the opening of King
Tutankhamen's tomb, Valley of the Kings, Egypt, November 1922

· ·

Directions Use the text on page 77 and the photograph to answer the questions. Write complete sentences.

1. Where and when was the photograph taken?

_____

_____

2. How do you think Howard Carter felt after uncovering this tomb that had been hidden for over 3,000 years?

_____

_____

3. Do you think the work of archaeologists is important? Tell why or why not.

_____

_____

GO ON ▶

Part B: Essay

Directions

Write a well-developed essay about ancient Egypt. Include an introduction, supporting paragraphs, and a conclusion. Use the documents on pages 71–78, your answers to the questions in Part A, and your knowledge of social studies to help you organize your ideas. Use your own paper to write the essay.

In your essay, remember to discuss:

- the accomplishments of the ancient Egyptians
- their religious beliefs
- the Pyramids and their purpose
- archaeology in Egypt

Directions

Use the space below to brainstorm. Then write your essay on your own paper.

Name _____ Date _____

Practice Test 2 ⋯⋯⋯⋯⋯⋯⋯⋯⋯⋯⋯⋯⋯⋯⋯⋯⋯⋯⋯⋯⋯

Directions This practice test is based on documents 1 through 3. It will test your ability to work with historical documents. In Part A, look at each document and answer the questions after it. Use your answers to the questions in Part A to help you write your essay in Part B.

Historical Background

> The Great Wall of China runs from the western city of Jiayuguan to the Yellow Sea. Between these points, the wall zigzags across 2,150 miles. Building the wall took 1,800 years and millions of laborers.
>
> Around 200 B.C., the Chinese emperor Shi Huangdi decided to build a wall to keep Mongolian barbarians out of China. The wall followed the land. It ran along rivers instead of across them and up hills rather than around them. By the end of Shi Huangdi's 15-year rule, about 1,200 miles of the wall had been completed.

• •

Directions For **Part A**, study EACH document carefully and answer the questions after it. These answers will help you write your essay.

For **Part B**, use the information from the documents, your answers from Part A, and your knowledge of social studies to write a well-organized essay. The focus of your essay will be the Great Wall of China.

The Great Wall of China

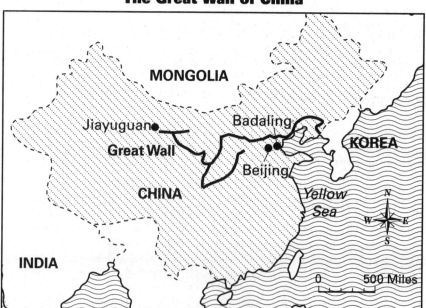

Unit 4: Test Practice with Document-Based Questions
Voices: World History, SV 9781419036392

Name _____ Date _____

Part A: Short-Answer Questions ·····················

 Directions | The following documents give information about the Great Wall of China. Study each document carefully. Then answer the questions that follow it.

Document 1

Source: National Archives and Records Administration

Troop L, 6th U.S. Cavalry, at the Great Wall of China, East of
Nan-Kow Pass, 1900

· ·

Directions | Use the photograph to answer the questions. Write complete sentences.

1. When and where was this photograph taken?

_____

2. Who are the horsemen in the photograph?

_____

_____

3. How does this photograph illustrate some of the details about the wall given in the historical background on page 80?

_____

_____

GO ON ▶

Name _____ Date _____

The description below was written by a visitor to China in 1795.

Document 2

The pyramids of Egypt are little, when compared with a wall which . . . stretches along an extent of fifteen hundred miles, and is of such an enormous thickness, that six horsemen may easily ride abreast upon it. . . . One third of the able bodied men of China were employed in constructing this wall, and the workmen were ordered, under pain of death, to place the materials of which it was composed so closely that the least entrance might not be left for any instrument of iron. . . .

The foundation consists of large blocks of square stones laid in mortar; but all the rest is constructed of bricks. The whole is so strong, and well built, that it scarcely needs any repairs. . . . When carried over steep rocks where no horse can pass, it is about fifteen or twenty feet high, and broad in proportion; but when running through a valley, or crossing a river, you behold a strong wall, about thirty feet high, with square towers at certain intervals. . . . The top of the wall is flat, and paved with cut stone; and where it rises over a rock or eminence, there is an ascent by easy stone stairs.

from *An Historical, Geographical, and Philosophical View of the Chinese Empire,* by William Winterbotham, 1795

. . . .

Directions | Use the reading selection to answer the questions. Write complete sentences.

1. How many people worked to build the Great Wall of China?

_____

2. What is the Great Wall of China made of?

_____

3. How tall is the Great Wall of China?

_____

GO ON ▶

Name _____ Date _____

The Great Wall served as a pathway as well as a barrier. Every 200 yards, a stairway was built on the Chinese side of the wall. Soldiers climbed the stairway to the top of the wall. In this way, they could rush to any part of the wall under attack.

The builders also included 25,000 watchtowers in the wall. Each tower housed 30 to 50 soldiers. In peacetime, the soldiers kept the wall repaired and oversaw the traders who entered through the wall's gates. During wartime, the soldiers drove off invaders with cannons atop the towers.

The diagram below shows some of these features and how the wall was constructed.

 Document 3

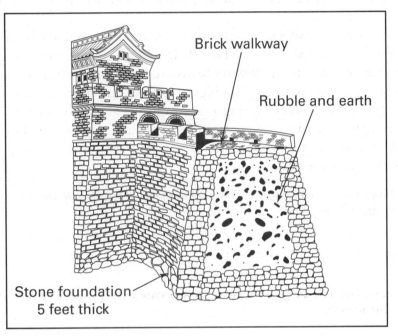

Brick walkway

Rubble and earth

Stone foundation
5 feet thick

. . . .

Directions / Use the information and the diagram to answer the questions. Write complete sentences.

1. How thick is the foundation of the Great Wall?

_____

2. What were the watchtowers used for?

_____

3. What was the purpose for building the Great Wall?

_____

_____

_____

GO ON ▶

Part B: Essay

Directions | **Write a well-developed essay about the Great Wall of China. Include an introduction, supporting paragraphs, and a conclusion. Use the documents on pages 81–83, your answers to the questions in Part A, and your knowledge of social studies to help you organize your ideas. Use your own paper to write the essay.**

In your essay, remember to discuss:

- what the Great Wall of China was
- where, when, and why the Great Wall was built
- the structure of the Great Wall
- how the Great Wall was used

Directions | **Use the space below to brainstorm. Then write your essay on your own paper.**

Practice Test 3 ··································

Directions This practice test is based on documents 1 through 7. It will test your ability to work with historical documents. In Part A, look at each document and answer the questions after it. Consider the context and point of view of each document. Use your answers to the questions in Part A to help you write your essay in Part B.

Historical Background

Until the 1840s, many women and children were employed in the coal mines of Great Britain. The work was backbreaking, and the working conditions were horrible. But hard economic times forced the women and children to seek such jobs. In 1842, Lord Ashley formed a commission to hear testimony about the practice. Parliament then passed the 1842 Mines Act. This act established new labor guidelines for British coal mines.

···

Directions For **Part A**, study EACH document carefully and answer the questions after it. These answers will help you write your essay.

For **Part B**, use the information from the documents, your answers from Part A, and your knowledge of social studies to write a well-organized essay. The focus of your essay will be British coal mines in the 1840s.

Girl pulling a coal tub in mine

GO ON ▶

Name _____ Date _____

Part A: Short-Answer Questions ···

Directions | The following documents show information about the British coal mines in the 1840s. Study each document carefully. Then answer the questions that follow it.

In the early 1800s, many young people and women had to work in the mines. The conditions were awful. Lord Ashley's Mines Commission of 1842 gathered testimony about the mines. The testimony below is from a 17-year-old girl. A hurrier is a person who pulled a coal tub, or corf, as shown in the illustration on page 85.

Document 1

> My father has been dead about a year; my mother is living and has ten children, five lads and five lasses. . . . All my sisters have been hurriers, but three went to the mill. Alice went because her legs swelled from hurrying in cold water when she was hot. I never went to day-school; I go to Sunday-school, but I cannot read or write; I go to pit at five o'clock in the morning and come out at five in the evening; I get my breakfast of porridge and milk first; I take my dinner with me, a cake, and eat it as I go; I do not stop or rest any time for the purpose; I get nothing else until I get home, and then have potatoes and meat, not every day meat. I hurry in the clothes I have now got on, trousers and ragged jacket; the bald place upon my head is made by thrusting the corves . . . I hurry the corves a mile and more under ground and back; they weigh [about 200 pounds]; I hurry 11 a-day.

from Patience Kershaw, testimony to Lord Ashley's Mines Commission, May 15, 1842

· ·

Directions | Use the testimony to answer the questions. Write complete sentences. Use another sheet of paper.

1. How many hours a day did Patience Kershaw work in the mine?

2. What was Patience Kershaw's job in the mine?

3. About how much coal did Patience Kershaw move in a day?

4. What can you tell about this person from the testimony?

5. What do you think working in the mines would be like? Would you want to work in the mines?

GO ON ▶

Hurriers, or drawers, had to pull or push heavy carts loaded with coal through narrow low tunnels of usually less than three feet high. The illustration shows these workers. The testimony tells of the horrible conditions of the job.

 ## Document 2

 ## Document 3

Robert North says, "I went into the pit at 7 years of age. When I drew by the girdle and chain, the skin was broken and the blood ran down. . . . If we said anything, they would beat us. I have seen many draw at 6. They must do it or be beat. They cannot straighten their backs during the day. I have sometimes pulled till my hips have hurt me so that I have not known what to do with myself."

from a speech by the Earl of Shaftesbury, June 1842

Directions | **Use the illustration and the testimony to answer the questions. Write complete sentences. Use another sheet of paper.**

1. How old was Robert North when he went to work in the mine?

2. What kinds of injuries did he suffer from the job?

3. What happened to him if he did not do his work well?

4. Based on the illustration, would you want to do this kind of job? Tell why or why not.

GO ON ▶

Name _____ Date _____

In 1845, Friedrich Engels wrote a book about working conditions in England. He included information on the terrible conditions in the mines.

Document 4

In the coal and iron mines which are worked in pretty much the same way, children of four, five, and seven years are employed. They are set to transporting the ore or coal loosened by the miner from its place to the horse-path or the main shaft, and to opening and shutting the doors (which separate the divisions of the mine and regulate its ventilation) for the passage of workers and material. For watching the doors the smallest children are usually employed, who thus pass twelve hours daily, in the dark, alone, sitting usually in damp passages without even having work enough to save them from the stupefying, brutalising tedium of doing nothing. The transport of coal and iron-stone, on the other hand, is very hard labour, the stuff being shoved in large tubs, without wheels, over the uneven floor of the mine; often over moist clay, or through water, and frequently up steep inclines and through paths so low-roofed that the workers are forced to creep on hands and knees. For this more wearing labour, therefore, older children and half-grown girls are employed. One man or two boys per tub are employed, according to circumstances; and, if two boys, one pushes and the other pulls.

from *The Condition of the Working Class in England in 1844*, by Friedrich Engels, 1845

. . . .

Directions Use the text excerpt to answer the questions. Write complete sentences. Use another sheet of paper.

1. What age worker was hired to open and close the doors of the mine?

2. Those who worked the doors were called trappers. What were the working conditions of this job?

3. How was the coal moved around in the mine?

4. Who was hired to do this kind of work?

5. Those who moved the tubs were called hurriers or drawers. What were the working conditions of this job?

GO ON ▶

The illustration and text portray another way the coal was carried out of the mine. Usually, women or older girls were given this job.

Document 5

Document 6

The tugs or straps are placed over the forehead, and the body bent in a semicircular form to strengthen the arch. Large lumps of coal are then placed upon her neck, and she commences her journey with her burden to the bottom, first hanging her lamp to the cloth crossing her forehead. She has first to travel eighty-four feet, from the wall face to the first ladder, which is eighteen feet high; leaving the first ladder, she proceeds along the main road, which is from three . . . to four . . . feet high, to the second ladder, eighteen feet high; so on to the third and fourth ladders, till she reaches the pit-bottom . . . where she casts her load, varying from a hundred to a hundred and fifty weight, in the tub. Add the length of the ladders ascended, and the distance along the "roads," and they exceed the height of St. Paul's Cathedral [365 feet]; and it not unfrequently happens that the tugs break and the load falls upon the females who are following.

from "Women in the British Mines," *The Ladies' Repository*, July 1854

· ·

Directions Use the illustration and the text excerpt to answer the questions. Write complete sentences. Use another sheet of paper.

1. How did the women in the reading selection move the coal?

2. Does this process sound like the most efficient way to move coal? Explain.

3. Imagine that you had the job described in the illustration and reading selection. What would a day in your life be like? Write a short narrative.

GO ON ▶

Lord Ashley's mine commission heard testimony about the deplorable conditions in the British mines in early 1842. Soon after, Parliament passed the 1842 Mines Act. The act restricted how women and children could be employed in the mines. The act was meant to help the mistreated female and child mine workers. But many of them were upset by the act because it meant that many of them no longer had jobs.

 ## Document 7

> **The 1842 Mines Act**
>
> • No female was to be employed underground.
>
> • No boy under 10 years old was to be employed underground.
>
> • Apprentices between the ages of 10 and 18 could continue to work in the mines.
>
> • There were no regulations relating to hours of work.

Directions **Use the information in the box to answer the questions. Write complete sentences.**

1. After the 1842 Mines Act was passed, who could no longer work underground?

_____

_____

2. Did the act include any limits on how many hours a person had to work?

_____

3. The 1842 Mines Act put many people out of work. Was the act a good one? Explain your answer.

_____

_____

_____

_____

_____

_____

_____

_____

GO ON ▶

Name _____ Date _____

Part B: Essay ···

Directions Write a well-developed essay about British coal mines in the 1840s. Include an introduction, supporting paragraphs, and a conclusion. Use the documents on pages 86–90, your answers to the questions in Part A, and your knowledge of social studies to help you organize your ideas. Use your own paper to write the essay.

> **In your essay, remember to discuss:**
> - why women and children worked in the mines
> - the kinds of jobs women and children did in the mines
> - the working conditions in the mines
> - legislation passed to solve the problems
> - the effect of the legislation

··

Directions Use the space below to brainstorm. Then write your essay on your own paper.

Practice Test 4 ....

Directions | This practice test is based on documents 1 through 7. It will test your ability to work with historical documents. In Part A, look at each document and answer the questions after it. Consider the context and point of view of each document. Use your answers to the questions in Part A to help you write your essay in Part B.

Historical Background

World War I was known as "the war to end all wars." It began in eastern Europe in the summer of 1914. First, a Serb man shot Austro-Hungarian Archduke Franz Ferdinand and his wife as they drove through the city of Sarajevo. Then, Austria-Hungary demanded justice and declared war on Serbia. Germany sided with Austria-Hungary, and Russia sided with Serbia. On August 1, Germany declared war on Russia, and the Great War had begun. The United States entered the war in 1917. In November 1918, World War I ended.

....

Directions | For **Part A**, study EACH document carefully and answer the questions after it. These answers will help you write your essay.

For **Part B**, use the information from the documents, your answers from Part A, and your knowledge of social studies to write a well-organized essay. The focus of your essay will be World War I.

Source: Sophia Smith Collection, Smith College

Doughboys (U.S. soldiers) watching German planes fly overhead during World War I

GO ON ▶

Name _____ Date _____

Part A: Short-Answer Questions ·······················

Directions | The following documents show information about World War I. Study each document carefully. Then answer the questions that follow it.

Austria-Hungary, Germany, and other countries were the Central Powers in World War I. Russia, the United Kingdom, the United States, and other countries were the Allies. Several countries in Europe were neutral. The map below shows the role of countries in World War I.

Document 1

Europe in World War I

Directions | Use the map to answer the questions. Write complete sentences.

1. Which side were Turkey and Bulgaria on in World War I?

_____

2. Which side were France and Italy on in World War I?

_____

3. What were two neutral countries in World War I?

_____

_____

4. Why do you think these nations thought war was necessary to solve their dispute?

_____

GO ON ▶

World War I was different from later wars. Many soldiers still rode horses in the war. Cars and airplanes were new inventions. But World War I quickly became a new kind of war for a new century.

 Document 2

Source: Courier-Journal and Louisville Times

Soldiers riding teams of horses at a World War I training camp in Kentucky

· ·

Directions   **Use the photograph to answer the questions. Write complete sentences.**

1. How are these soldiers different from soldiers in later wars?

_____

_____

2. Do you think that war is a good way to settle disputes? Tell why or why not.

_____

_____

_____

_____

_____

_____

GO ON ▶

German submarines, or U-boats, began to sink ships in the Atlantic Ocean. On May 7, 1915, the passenger ship *Lusitania* was sunk by a German U-boat. Many Americans died when the ship was torpedoed. Below is part of the war diary of the captain of the German submarine that sank the *Lusitania*.

Document 3

2 p.m. Straight ahead the 4 funnels and 2 masts of a steamer were visible. . . . Ship is made out to be a large passenger steamer.

3:10 p.m. Clear bow shot at 700 m. . . . Shot struck starboard side close behind the bridge. An extraordinarily heavy detonation followed, with a very large cloud of smoke. A second explosion must have followed that of the torpedo (boiler or coal or powder!). The superstructure above the point of impact and the bridge were torn apart; fire broke out; light smoke veiled the high bridge. The ship stopped immediately and quickly listed sharply to starboard, sinking deeper by the head at the same time. It appeared as if it would capsize in a short time. Great confusion arose on the ship; some of the boats were swung clear and lowered into the water. . . . The ship blew off steam; at the bow the name "Lusitania" in golden letters was visible.

3:25 p.m. Since it seemed the steamer could only remain above water a short time, went to 24 m. and ran to the Sea. Nor could I have fired a second torpedo into this swarm of people who were trying to save themselves.

4:15 p.m. Went to 11 m. and took a look around. In the distance straight ahead a number of life-boats were moving; nothing more was to be seen of the "Lusitania."

Source: German Submarine U-20 war diary by Lieutenant Walter Schwieger, National Archives and Records Administration, 1915

· ·

Directions | Use the diary entry to answer the questions. Write complete sentences. Use another sheet of paper.

1. What happened to the *Lusitania* when the torpedo struck it?

2. How did the passengers on the *Lusitania* react to the explosion?

3. Why do you think the U-boat captain decided to fire upon a passenger ship?

4. Does your feeling about the U-boat captain change after he says he could not fire a second torpedo into the swarm of people trying to save themselves? Explain.

GO ON ▶

Name _____ Date _____

After the sinking of the *Lusitania*, German U-boats sank other ships, some of them American. Finally, in 1917 President Woodrow Wilson called on Congress to declare war against Germany. On April 6, 1917, the United States entered World War I on the side of the Allies. The cartoon below shows Wilson planning his call for war. The cartoon was drawn by Clifford Berryman and appeared on March 21, 1917.

 Document 4

President calls Congress April 2 to act on grave national policy

. . . .

Directions   **Use the cartoon to answer the questions. Write complete sentences.**

1. Based on the cartoon, what was President Wilson's reason for asking Congress to declare war?

_____

_____

_____

2. Do you think President Wilson was right to ask Congress to declare war? Tell why or why not.

_____

_____

_____

_____

GO ON ▶

Name _____ Date _____

Many young men went to war with a sense of glory. However, once in battle, they found there was little glory to be had. Instead, they found fatigue, poison gas, and death. The chart below shows the total losses in soldiers, civilians, and money during World War I.

 **Document 5**

Total Losses in World War I

	Total Number of Soldiers	Dead in Battle	Civilians Dead	Financial Cost in $ Millions
Central Powers	19,650,000	3,131,889	3,485,000	86,238
Allies	42,188,810	4,888,891	3,157,633	193,367

Directions   Use the chart to answer the questions. Write complete sentences.

1. The two sides in World War I were called the Allies and the Central Powers. Which side had the greater number of soldiers?

_____

2. How many soldiers of the Allies were killed in World War I?

_____

_____

3. Which side had more civilians killed?

_____

_____

4. The Allies won the war. Based on the chart, which side had the greater total losses during the war? Explain using evidence from the chart.

_____

_____

_____

_____

_____

_____

_____

_____

GO ON ▶

Name _____ Date _____

Several young men known as the Trench Poets wrote about their experiences in World War I. Wilfred Owen, whose poem appears below, was one of them. Owen died in the war in 1918, a week before its end. The "old Lie" Owen mentions in the end of the poem comes from Latin and means "It is sweet and right to die for your country."

Document 6

Dulce Et Decorum Est

Bent double, like old beggars under sacks,
Knock-kneed, coughing like hags, we cursed through sludge,
Till on the haunting flares we turned our backs
And towards our distant rest began to trudge.
Men marched asleep. Many had lost their boots
But limped on, blood-shod. All went lame; all blind;
Drunk with fatigue . . .

GAS! Gas! Quick, boys!—An ecstasy of fumbling,
Fitting the clumsy helmets just in time;
But someone still was yelling out and stumbling
And floundering like a man in fire or lime.—
Dim, through the misty panes and thick green light
As under a green sea, I saw him drowning. . . .

If in some smothering dreams you too could pace
Behind the wagon that we flung him in,
And watch the white eyes writhing in his face, . . .
If you could hear, at every jolt, the blood
Come gargling from the froth-corrupted lungs, . . .
My friend, you would not tell with such high zest
To children ardent for some desperate glory,
The old Lie: Dulce et decorum est
Pro patria mori.

Wilfred Owen, 1917

• •

Directions **Use the poem to answer the questions. Write complete sentences. Use another sheet of paper.**

1. Does Owen's description of war sound glorious or awful? Explain.

2. What images does Owen use to portray the gas attack?

3. Is Owen's poem for or against war? Explain your answer.

4. Owen's poem says the idea that it is glorious to die in war for your country is a lie. Do you agree or disagree? Explain.

GO ON

Name _____ Date _____

In World War I, civilians were called upon to support the war effort. Many women entered the workforce to take the place of men who had gone to war. Another way civilians could help the war effort was to buy war bonds or victory bonds. The poster below was issued by the Victory Bond Committee of Canada in 1917.

Document 7

Victory Bond Committee, Canada, 1917

Source: National Archives and Records Administration

....

Directions Use the poster to answer the questions. Write complete sentences. Use another sheet of paper.

1. What does the poster try to make people do?

2. Do you think the poster is effective? Tell why or why not.

3. Do citizens have an obligation to support a war effort? Explain your answer.

GO ON ▶

Part B: Essay ···

Directions

Write a well-developed essay about World War I. Include an introduction, supporting paragraphs, and a conclusion. Use the documents on pages 93–99, your answers to the questions in Part A, and your knowledge of social studies to help you organize your ideas. Use your own paper to write the essay.

> **In your essay, remember to discuss:**
>
> • when and why World War I started
>
> • when and why the United States entered the war
>
> • how World War I was different from other wars
>
> • the losses caused by the war
>
> • how civilians participated in the war effort

···

Directions

Use the space below to brainstorm. Then write your essay on your own paper.

Practice Test 5 ···

Directions | This practice test is based on documents 1 through 8. It will test your ability to work with historical documents. In Part A, look at each document and answer the questions after it. Use your answers to the questions in Part A to help you write your essay in Part B.

Historical Background

> During the late 1950s and through the 1960s, the United States and the Soviet Union were engaged in the Space Race. Each nation wanted to lead the way in space exploration. The competition provided scientific knowledge about our solar system. It also led to humans on the moon. The Space Race began in 1957 when the Soviet Union launched the first artificial satellite, *Sputnik*. It ended when U.S. astronauts landed on the moon on July 20, 1969.

· ·

Directions | For **Part A**, study EACH document carefully and answer the questions after it. These answers will help you write your essay.

For **Part B**, use the information from the documents, your answers from Part A, and your knowledge of social studies to write a well-organized essay. The focus of your essay will be the Space Race between the United States and the Soviet Union.

Source: National Archives and Records Administration

The moon from *Apollo 8*, 1968

GO ON ▶

Name _____ Date _____

Part A: Short-Answer Questions ·······················

Directions The following documents give information about the **Space Race** between the United States and the Soviet Union in the 1950s and 1960s. Study each document carefully. Then answer the questions that follow it.

Document 1

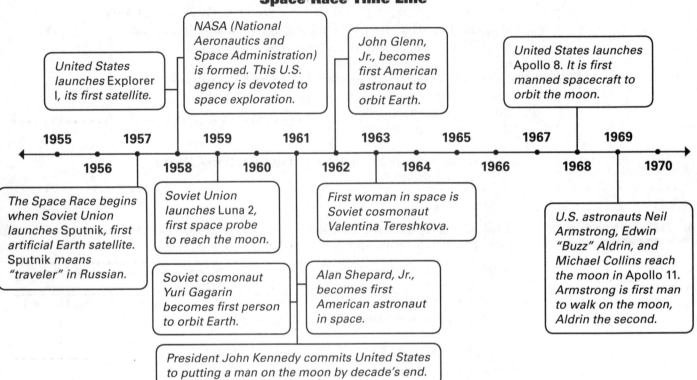

Space Race Time Line

NASA (National Aeronautics and Space Administration) is formed. This U.S. agency is devoted to space exploration.

United States launches Explorer I, *its first satellite.*

John Glenn, Jr., becomes first American astronaut to orbit Earth.

United States launches Apollo 8. *It is first manned spacecraft to orbit the moon.*

1955   1957   1959   1961   1963   1965   1967   1969

1956   1958   1960   1962   1964   1966   1968   1970

The Space Race begins when Soviet Union launches Sputnik, *first artificial Earth satellite.* Sputnik *means "traveler" in Russian.*

Soviet Union launches Luna 2, *first space probe to reach the moon.*

First woman in space is Soviet cosmonaut Valentina Tereshkova.

U.S. astronauts Neil Armstrong, Edwin "Buzz" Aldrin, and Michael Collins reach the moon in Apollo 11. Armstrong is first man to walk on the moon, Aldrin the second.

Soviet cosmonaut Yuri Gagarin becomes first person to orbit Earth.

Alan Shepard, Jr., becomes first American astronaut in space.

President John Kennedy commits United States to putting a man on the moon by decade's end.

·······················

Directions Use the time line to answer the questions. Write complete sentences. Use a separate sheet of paper.

1. When did the Space Race begin?

2. Who was the first person in space?

3. Who was the first woman in space?

4. Which country won the Space Race? Explain your answer.

5. Would you like to fly to the moon? Tell why or why not.

GO ON ▶

President John F. Kennedy believed strongly in the space program. In 1961, he gave a speech to Congress. He called on Congress and the nation to make a commitment—to send a manned space flight to the moon! In 1963, President Kennedy was assassinated in Dallas, Texas. But his dream of men on the moon came true in the summer of 1969.

Document 2

First, I believe that this nation should commit itself to achieving the goal, before this decade is out, of landing a man on the moon and returning him safely to the earth. No single space project in this period will be more impressive to mankind, or more important for the long-range exploration of space; and none will be so difficult or expensive to accomplish.

from President John Kennedy's speech to Congress, May 21, 1961

Directions Use the speech excerpt to answer the questions. Write complete sentences.

1. When did President Kennedy want to land a man on the moon?

_____

_____

2. If you were president, what commitment would you ask for from the nation?

_____

_____

3. Do you think space exploration is important? Explain your answer.

_____

_____

_____

_____

_____

_____

_____

_____

_____

GO ON ▶

Name _____ Date _____

The Mercury program was NASA's first attempt to put men into space. Only one man made the trip into space each time. In the photograph below, President John Kennedy and John Glenn, Jr., look into a Mercury capsule, *Friendship 7*. John Glenn, Jr., was the first American to orbit Earth. He rode the capsule around Earth three times in a five-hour flight.

Document 3

Source: National Archives and Records Administration

President Kennedy inspects interior of *Friendship 7*, Cape Canaveral, Florida, Hangar S, February 23, 1962

. . . .

Directions Use the photograph to answer the questions. Write complete sentences.

1. Based on the picture, how big do you think *Friendship 7* was? Give measurements.

_____

2. Do you think you would like to orbit Earth in such a small spacecraft? How do you think Astronaut Glenn felt?

_____

_____

3. What do you think the inside of the capsule looks like? What would be needed to send a person into space? On another sheet of paper, draw a picture of the interior of a space capsule. (Remember, the capsule is the tip of a big rocket. The capsule does not have rocket engines.)

GO ON ▶

Unit 4: Test Practice with Document-Based Questions
Voices: World History, SV 9781419036392

Many people mistakenly think that Sally Ride was the first woman in space. She was the first American woman in space. But the first woman in space was from the Soviet Union. On June 16, 1963, Valentina Tereshkova was launched into space. The name of her spacecraft was *Vostok 6*. Tereshkova made 48 orbits of Earth and spent almost three days in space. She was 26 years old.

 Document 4

Source: Library of Congress

Cosmonaut Valentina Tereshkova, 1963

Quotes from Valentina Tereshkova

• If women can be railroad workers in Russia, why can't they fly in space?

• Once you've been in space, you appreciate how small and fragile the earth is.

. . . .

Directions   **Write complete sentences to answer the questions.**

1. Who was the first woman in space?

_____

2. When did her flight launch?

_____

3. In her second quote, Tereshkova talks about having been in space. What is the effect of being in space?

_____

GO ON ▶

105

Name _____ Date _____

In the early 1960s, D. Brainerd Holmes, Director of Manned Space Flight Programs, NASA, wrote a series of articles. He discussed the agency's plans to send astronauts into space. In the excerpt below, he wrote about landing a man on the moon.

Document 5

The first man on the moon will survey a bleak domain. Since there is no atmosphere to screen out solar radiation, the lunar explorers will have to wear protective suits at all times. The absence of an atmosphere, however, makes the moon so attractive as a place for scientific observations by man. . . .

But these . . . scientific advantages are not the chief reasons that propel man outward into space. The motivation for manned space flight goes deeper. Throughout history, man's destiny has compelled him to explore the unknown, scale every summit, overcome every obstacle.

The means to reach the moon are almost within man's grasp. But this will only be the beginning. Beyond the moon are the planets of this solar system and then other solar systems.

Source: National Archives and Records Administration
D. Brainerd Holmes, "The Future of Manned Space Flights," 1962

• •

Directions Use the article excerpt to answer the questions. Write complete sentences.

1. According to the article, what kind of environment can an astronaut expect on the moon?

_____

_____

2. What does the author say causes people to want to fly in space?

_____

_____

_____

3. Would you want to fly in space? Tell why or why not.

_____

_____

_____

_____

_____

GO ON ▶

Name _____ Date _____

In 1968, *Apollo 8* reached and orbited the moon, but it did not land. A year later, *Apollo 11* landed on the moon.

Document 6

Source: NASA

Apollo 11 landing in crater on the moon, July 1969

"Houston, Tranquility base here. The eagle has landed."

from Transmission from the moon, July 20, 1969

Directions   **Use the photograph and the transmission to answer the questions. Write complete sentences.**

1. Why do you think the transmission says the "eagle has landed"? What is the eagle?

_____

_____

2. How do you think the astronauts felt as they landed on the moon?

_____

_____

_____

_____

GO ON ▶

On July 20, 1969, *Apollo 11* landed on the moon. A few hours later, Neil Armstrong stepped out onto the surface of the moon. As he did, he described the accomplishment as "one small step for a man—one giant leap for mankind." A few minutes later, Edwin "Buzz" Aldrin joined Armstrong on the surface of the moon. A flag was planted, and a plaque was placed on the surface of the moon. Armstrong took the photograph below of Aldrin near the flag.

Document 7

Source: NASA

Astronaut Edwin Aldrin poses for a photo beside the flag of the United States. The astronauts' footprints in the soil of the moon are clearly visible in the foreground.

> The plaque reads:
>
> "Here men from the planet Earth first set foot on the moon July 1969, A.D. We came in peace for all mankind."

. . . .

Directions | Use the photograph and the plaque to answer the questions. Write complete sentences.

1. What would you say if you were the first person on the moon?

_____

2. Was landing men on the moon an important accomplishment? Tell why or why not.

_____

GO ON ▶

Name _____ Date _____

Six *Apollo* missions landed on the moon. The graph below shows how long each mission stayed on the surface of the moon.

Document 8

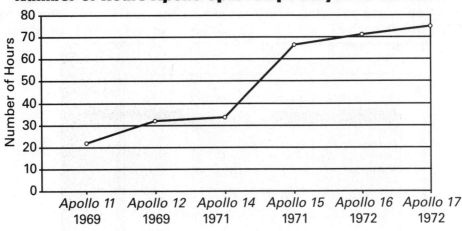

Number of Hours *Apollo* Spaceships Stayed on the Moon

1. How many hours did *Apollo 11* stay on the moon?

_____

2. How many hours did *Apollo 15* stay on the moon?

_____

3. Which *Apollo* spaceship stayed on the moon the longest?

_____

4. What do you notice about the amount of time each later *Apollo* spaceship stayed on the moon?

_____

_____

5. Do you think new missions to the moon should be planned? Tell why or why not.

_____

_____

_____

_____

GO ON ▶

Name _____ Date _____

Part B: Essay ···

Directions Write a well-developed essay about the Space Race between the United States and the Soviet Union in the 1950s and 1960s. Include an introduction, supporting paragraphs, and a conclusion. Use the documents on pages 102–109, your answers to the questions in Part A, and your knowledge of social studies to help you organize your ideas. Use your own paper to write the essay.

In your essay, remember to discuss:

- when and why the Space Race started
- the goal of the Space Race
- some of the highlights of the Space Race
- *Apollo 11*'s landing on the moon
- later *Apollo* missions to the moon

Directions Use the space below to brainstorm. Then write your essay on your own paper.

Practice Test 6 ···

Directions This practice test is based on documents 1 through 6. It will test your ability to work with historical documents. In Part A, look at each document and answer the questions after it. Use your answers to the questions in Part A to help you write your essay in Part B.

Historical Background

> The Great Wall of China was built to keep people out. The Berlin Wall was built to keep people in. It was built to keep people from leaving East Germany. After World War II, Germany was split. The Soviet Union controlled East Germany, and the United States and other countries controlled West Germany. The city of Berlin itself was split. In 1961, the East German government erected the wall to keep East Berlin people from escaping to democratic West Berlin. The Berlin Wall became a symbol of the cold war. The wall was finally opened in 1989.

· ·

Directions For **Part A**, study EACH document carefully and answer the questions after it. These answers will help you write your essay.

For **Part B**, use the information from the documents, your answers from Part A, and your knowledge of social studies to write a well-organized essay. The focus of your essay will be the Berlin Wall.

Berlin After World War II

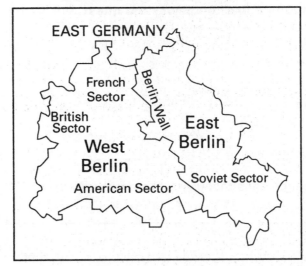

111

GO ON ▶

Name _____ Date _____

Part A: Short-Answer Questions ················

Directions | The following documents give information about the Berlin Wall. Study each document carefully. Then answer the questions that follow it.

The time line below shows important events in the history of the Berlin Wall.

 Document 1

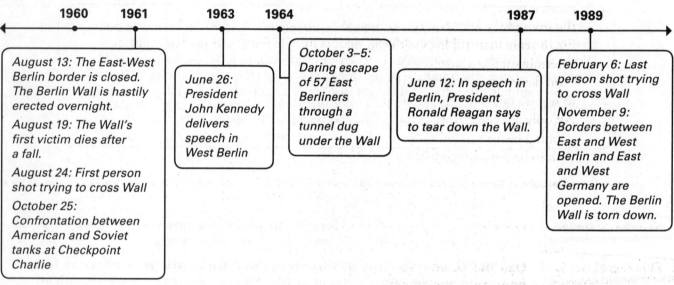

1960   1961   1963   1964   1987   1989

August 13: The East-West Berlin border is closed. The Berlin Wall is hastily erected overnight.

August 19: The Wall's first victim dies after a fall.

August 24: First person shot trying to cross Wall

October 25: Confrontation between American and Soviet tanks at Checkpoint Charlie

June 26: President John Kennedy delivers speech in West Berlin

October 3–5: Daring escape of 57 East Berliners through a tunnel dug under the Wall

June 12: In speech in Berlin, President Ronald Reagan says to tear down the Wall.

February 6: Last person shot trying to cross Wall

November 9: Borders between East and West Berlin and East and West Germany are opened. The Berlin Wall is torn down.

· ·

Directions | Use the time line to answer the questions. Write complete sentences.

1. When was the Berlin Wall erected?

_____

2. When was the Berlin Wall torn down?

_____

3. When were the first and last persons shot trying to cross the Wall?

_____

_____

4. How do you think Berliners felt when they awoke to find they could no longer visit their friends in the same city? How would you feel?

_____

_____

GO ON ▶

On June 26, 1963, U.S. President John F. Kennedy visited West Berlin. He gave a speech condemning the Berlin Wall. Part of his speech is below.

Document 2

Freedom has many difficulties and democracy is not perfect, but we have never had to put a wall up to keep our people in, to prevent them from leaving us. I want to say, on behalf of my countrymen, who live many miles away on the other side of the Atlantic, who are far distant from you, that they take the greatest pride that they have been able to share with you, even from a distance, the story of the last 18 years. I know of no town, no city, that has been besieged for 18 years that still lives with the vitality and the force, and the hope and the determination of the city of West Berlin. While the wall is the most obvious and vivid demonstration of the failures of the Communist system, for all the world to see, we take no satisfaction in it, for it is, as your Mayor has said, an offense not only against history but an offense against humanity, separating families, dividing husbands and wives and brothers and sisters, and dividing a people who wish to be joined together.

from John F. Kennedy's speech, Rudolph Wilde Platz, Berlin, West Germany, June 26, 1963

- -

Directions **Use the speech excerpt to answer the questions. Write complete sentences.**

1. Where and when did President Kennedy deliver this speech?

_____

2. President Kennedy said that the Wall showed the failures of Communism. What do you think he meant by that remark?

_____

_____

3. President Kennedy called the Berlin Wall an "offense against humanity." What do you think he meant by that remark?

_____

_____

GO ON ▶

Overnight, the Berlin Wall separated friends from friends and neighbors from neighbors. Families were also divided by the Wall. Many people died trying to cross the Wall. The photograph below shows the barrier topped by barbed wire.

 Document 3

Source: Library of Congress

People looking over the Berlin Wall

· ·

Directions / Use the photograph to answer the questions. Write complete sentences.

1. Why do you think people wanted to escape from East Berlin?

_____

_____

2. How do you think these people felt being separated from their friends and relatives on the other side of the Wall?

_____

_____

_____

_____

_____

_____

GO ON ▶

On June 12, 1987, U.S. President Ronald Reagan gave a speech in West Berlin. He delivered his speech at the Brandenburg Gate in the Berlin Wall. He called upon the leader of the Soviet Union, Mikhail Gorbachev, to tear down the Berlin Wall. Two years later, the Berlin Wall was torn down.

Document 4

Behind me stands a wall that encircles the free sectors of this city, part of a vast system of barriers that divides the entire continent of Europe. From the Baltic, south, those barriers cut across Germany in a gash of barbed wire, concrete, dog runs, and guard towers. Farther south, there may be no visible, no obvious wall. But there remain armed guards and checkpoints all the same—still a restriction on the right to travel, still an instrument to impose upon ordinary men and women the will of a totalitarian state. Yet it is here in Berlin where the wall emerges most clearly; here, cutting across your city, where the news photo and the television screen have imprinted this brutal division of a continent upon the mind of the world. Standing before the Brandenburg Gate, every man is a German, separated from his fellow men. Every man is a Berliner, forced to look upon a scar.

General Secretary Gorbachev, if you seek peace, if you seek prosperity for the Soviet Union and Eastern Europe, if you seek liberalization: Come here to this gate! Mr. Gorbachev, open this gate! Mr. Gorbachev, tear down this wall!

from Ronald Reagan's speech, Brandenburg Gate, Berlin, West Germany, June 12, 1987

. . . .

Directions   **Use the speech excerpt to answer the questions. Write complete sentences. Use another sheet of paper.**

1. Where and when did President Reagan deliver this speech?

2. President Reagan says that people in Berlin are forced to look upon a scar. What do you think he means by that remark?

3. What reasons does President Reagan give for Secretary Gorbachev to tear down the Berlin Wall?

GO ON ▶

Name _____ Date _____

The map below shows the areas controlled by the Soviet Union in Eastern Europe in 1989. In November 1989, the Berlin Wall was torn down. Slowly, one by one, Communist governments were overthrown. In December 1991, the Soviet Union itself fell.

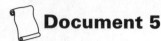 **Document 5**

Eastern Europe, 1989

. . . .

Directions   **Use the map to answer the questions. Write complete sentences.**

1. The nations that are not shaded were ruled by Communists in 1989. Was Czechoslovakia a Communist or noncommunist country?

_____

2. Name a country that was noncommunist in 1989.

_____

3. Based on the map, would you say that, in 1989, most of Eastern Europe was Communist or noncommunist?

_____

_____

4. Communist governments began to fall in 1989. Why do you think people in Eastern Europe grew tired of Communist rule?

_____

_____

_____

GO ON ▶

Unit 4: Test Practice with Document-Based Questions
Voices: World History, SV 9781419036392

Name _____ Date _____

On November 7, 1989, the East German government fell. On November 9, 1989, the Berlin Wall was opened. Crowds gathered to hammer the Wall, breaking it into pieces. East Germans were once again free to travel anywhere. The photograph below shows crowds of East Berliners and West Berliners mixing at Brandenburg Gate.

Document 6

Crowds at the Brandenburg Gate, November 9, 1989

Source: German Information Center

· ·

Directions   Use the photograph to answer the questions. Write complete sentences.

1. Where and when was this photograph taken?

_____

2. How do you think the people in the photograph felt about being able to travel through the Wall after 28 years?

_____

_____

3. Contrast the people in this photograph to the people in the photograph on page 114. How do you think the people in the two photographs are different?

_____

_____

GO ON ▶

Part B: Essay ··

Directions   Write a well-developed essay about the Berlin Wall. Include an introduction, supporting paragraphs, and a conclusion. Use the documents on pages 112–117, your answers to the questions in Part A, and your knowledge of social studies to help you organize your ideas. Use your own paper to write the essay.

> **In your essay, remember to discuss:**
> • when and why the Berlin Wall was built
> • political reactions to the Wall
> • how people in Germany must have felt when the Wall was built and when it was torn down

Directions   Use the space below to brainstorm. Then write your essay on your own paper.

Name _____ Date _____

Written Document Worksheet

OBSERVATION

Type of Document (Check one):

☐ Excerpt from Book or Magazine

☐ Newspaper

☐ Speech

☐ Advertisement

☐ Letter

☐ Telegram

☐ Government Document

☐ Congressional Record or Testimony

☐ Press Release

☐ Memorandum

☐ Report

☐ Other

Date of Document

Author or Creator of the Document

INTERPRETATION

List three important details or facts from the document.

_____

_____

_____

What is the purpose of the document? Why do you think this document was written?

What evidence in the document helps you understand the purpose? Use quotes from the document.

Who is the target audience of the document?

List two things the document tells about life in the United States at the time it was written.

_____

_____

Write a brief summary of the document.

QUESTIONS

Are there any questions you have not had answered by the document?

Where could you find answers to these questions?

Map Worksheet

OBSERVATION

Type of Map (Check one or more):

☐ Political Map   ☐ Region Map   ☐ Weather Map

☐ Historical Map   ☐ Resource Map   ☐ Events or Attractions Map

☐ Population Map   ☐ Landform Map   ☐ Elevation Map

☐ Route or Highway Map   ☐ Rivers or Waterways Map   ☐ Other

Unique Features of the Map (Check one or more):

☐ Title   ☐ Legend (key)   ☐ Latitude-Longitude Grid

☐ Compass Rose   ☐ Distance Scale   ☐ Other

Date of the Map

INTERPRETATION

List three details in this map you think are important.

_____

_____

_____

What is the purpose of the map? Why do you think the map was drawn?

What evidence in the map helps you understand the purpose?

Does the information in this map support or not support information that you have read? Explain.

QUESTIONS

Are there any questions you have not had answered by the map?

Name _____ Date _____

Photograph Worksheet

OBSERVATION

Study the photograph for two minutes. Form an overall impression of the photograph, and then examine individual items. Next, divide the photo into four equal sections and study each section to see what new details become visible.

Use the chart to list people, objects, and events in the photograph.

People	Objects	Events

INTERPRETATION

Based on what you have observed, list three things you can conclude from this photograph.

_____

_____

_____

How does the photograph affect you or make you feel?

QUESTIONS

What questions does this photograph raise for you?

Where could you find answers to these questions?

Political Cartoon Worksheet

OBSERVATION

List the objects or people in the cartoon.

Identify the cartoon caption or title.

Record any important dates or numbers in the cartoon.

Describe the action taking place in the cartoon.

INTERPRETATION

Are any of the people or objects in your list labeled? What do those labels mean?

Are any of the people or objects in your list symbols? What do they represent?

Which words or phrases in the cartoon are the most important? Explain.

List adjectives that describe emotions portrayed in the cartoon.

What is the message of the cartoon?

Is the cartoon effective in presenting its message?

Which special-interest groups might agree or disagree with the cartoon's message? Why?

QUESTIONS

What questions do you have about the cartoon?

How would you have drawn the cartoon differently?

Answer Key

Page 9

Answers may vary. Accept reasonable responses.

1. Answers will vary.
2. In this article, *picturesque* means charming or pretty in appearance.
3. Entrails are internal parts, especially bowels. Scoriae are the refuse from the melting of metals.
4. *Dilapidated* means decaying or falling apart.
5. Answers will vary.

Page 10

1. The Third Punic War was the shortest war.
2. The Second Punic War was fought to control lands in Spain.
3. One result of the Third Punic War was that Rome gained control of the Mediterranean Sea. OR One result of the Third Punic War was that Carthage was destroyed.

Page 11

1. The Fall of the Roman Empire occurred in 476.
2. Charlemagne became Emperor of the Holy Roman Empire in 800.
3. Christian Crusaders captured Jerusalem in 1099.
4. Check that the date and event are correctly placed and labeled.
5. Between Charlemagne being crowned and Martin Luther nailing his list to the door was a period of 717 years.

Page 12

1. D
2. C
3. D
4. B

Page 13

1. The value of gold produced in Mexico in 1907–1908 was 40 million pesos.
2. The value of silver was about 30 million pesos in 1882–1883.
3. Silver had a greater value during the time shown on the graph.
4. The most people in Europe now follow the Catholic religion.
5. Five percent of the people in Europe are Muslims.

Page 14

1. Cairo
2. Red Sea
3. Kuwait City is closer; about 400 miles
4. about 1,500 km
5. Tigris River and Euphrates River
6. Syria, Turkey, Iraq, and Iran

Page 15

1. Fascist
2. Democratic
3. Fascist
4. Soviet Union
5. Students should name two of these: Spain, Portugal, Greece, Turkey, Yugoslavia, Romania, Poland.

Page 16

Answers may vary. Accept reasonable responses.

1. The poster tells people to save a loaf of bread a week.
2. The loaf of bread probably represents food.
3. Answers will vary.

Page 17

1. September 7, 1940
2. large clouds of smoke
3. Answers will vary.

Page 18

1. Adolf Hitler
2. Germany
3. "Paper Packs a Punch—Save It!!!" The main idea is that people should recycle waste paper.

Page 19

Answers may vary. Accept reasonable responses.

1. Confucius refers to the prince in the quote.
2. The first sentence means that if the leader acts correctly, people will follow him without needing orders to do so.
3. The second sentence means that if the leader does not act correctly, people will not follow him even if he gives orders to do so.
4. The main idea is that a leader who acts correctly will have the trust and respect of his people.
5. Answers will vary.

Page 20

1. The tablet was written in 1780 B.C.
2. *Anonymous* means that the author is unknown.
3. Answers will vary.

Page 21

1. the widow Comon
2. on July 13, 1699
3. on July 24, 1699
4. The widow Comon was considered to be a witch and was killed.
5. Answers will vary.

Page 22

1. Answers will vary.
2. The trebuchet or trebucket form of ducking machine is described in the passage.
3. The ducking machine was locked up when not in use so that the village children would not play with it and duck each other.

Page 23

1. Frank Hazenplug drew the illustration.
2. The illustration was first published in 1896.
3. Answers will vary.
4. Answers will vary.
5. Answers will vary.

Page 24

1. The largest group of nations was the Allies.
2. *Neutral* means not taking sides. Students should name one of the following: Switzerland, Sweden, Spain, Portugal, Turkey, Ireland.
3. Germany, Italy, and Japan were called the Axis countries.
4. Students should name three of the following: United States, Great Britain, France, Soviet Union, China, Australia, Canada, Mexico.

Page 25

1. Thomas Edison invented the light bulb in 1879.
2. The effect of Henry Ford's invention was that people could travel in cars instead of on horses or on foot.
3. Answers may vary. Garrett Morgan's invention was important because it allowed traffic to move more safely.
4. Answers will vary.

Page 26

1. The first laser was built in 1960.
2. In 1666, Sir Isaac Newton discovered that white light is made up of all colors.
3. In 1590, the microscope was invented, and in 1609, Galileo built a telescope. Answers will vary on the importance of these inventions.
4. Answers will vary.

Page 27

1. About five million U.S. households burned wood as the main fuel in 1981.
2. The most households burned wood as the main fuel in 1984.
3. After 1984, the number of households using wood declined sharply.
4. Answers will vary.

Page 28

1. about 890 million
2. about 1985
3. no
4. Students will probably say yes. The graph shows that India had a population of about 1 billion in 2000. If it grows at the same rate, it could reach 1.5 billion by 2010.

Page 29

1. C
2. D
3. C
4. D

Page 30

1. 35%
2. 65%
3. increased
4. Yes, imports and exports changed. In 2006, Japan imported less from the United States and exported more to the United States than it did in 1997.

Page 31

1. 1914
2. cotton
3. Liberia, Belgian Congo, South Africa
4. South Africa
5. west

Page 32

Students should circle the named parts of the map.
1. desert climate
2. 0–2
3. tropical climate
4. southeast part
5. Answers may vary, but students should point out that the area has a temperate climate, which might be more attractive to more people.

Page 33

1. The central image is a group of small children sitting in front of their bombed home.
2. Answers will vary. The children are probably sad or upset.
3. Answers will vary.
4. Answers will vary.
5. Answers will vary.

Page 34

Answers may vary. Accept reasonable responses.
1. The woman represents the Statue of Liberty.
2. The image on the shield is an eagle. It represents the United States.
3. The words on the sword are "Be prepared." Answers will vary, but students might answer that the nation and its citizens should be prepared.
4. Answers will vary.
5. Answers will vary.

Page 36

Answers may vary. Accept reasonable responses.
1. The storm represents the battle for freedom, or World War II.
2. Answers will vary.
3. The main idea is that freedom must be fought for.
4. Answers will vary.

Page 37

Answers may vary. Accept reasonable responses.
1. The plague attacked people without warning, mostly the healthy. It struck all classes of people except a rich few.
2. People who got the plague died sometimes within a few hours, and surely in three or four days.
3. The statement means that the people died.

Page 38

1. Answers will vary but might include *exiled*, *proceed*, and *peers*.
2. Answers will vary.
3. The rights in the two documents are similar. The rights say that a person is safe within his person and property unless tried in a court for an offense.

Page 39

1. Answers will vary.
2. An inclination is a person's natural disposition or character—the way a person is.
3. A knick-knack is a trivial object usually used as an ornament.
4. Answers will vary but could suggest that, as a youth, Newton showed a keen interest in the way things worked.
5. Answers will vary.

Page 40

1. Most of these rights suggest a freedom of speech, especially 1, 4, and 10.
2. Law is the "expression of the general will."
3. Liberty is the freedom to do something as long as it does not injure another person. Liberty ends when its expression becomes harmful to another person.
4. Right 7 is the most similar to the rights discussed on page 38.

Page 41

1. Answers will vary. Accept responses that refer to the speech.
2.–4. Answers will vary.

Page 42

1. Brazil
2. Japan
3. Answers will vary. Accept responses that refer to the chart.
4. Answers will vary.

Page 43

1. Anglo-French War
2. Boxer Rebellion
3. 1912
4. Answers will vary but should suggest the Chinese had to keep fighting because they were winning the wars.

Page 44

1. Ramses II was the most recent ruler.
2. Amenhotep I was the most warlike ruler because he kept attacking neighboring countries to build his empire.
3. Hatshepsut was the only female ruler.
4. Ramses II made peace with his neighbors and started a massive building program.

Page 45

1. C
2. B
3. A
4. B
5. Answers will vary but might suggest that the independence movement occurred fairly quickly, lasting around 20 years.

Page 46

1. Italy surrendered to the Allies in 1943.
2. France surrendered to Germany in 1940.
3. *Neutrality* means that a country does not take sides in a conflict.
4. The United States entered the war after Japan attacked Pearl Harbor.
5. The surrenders of Germany and Japan in 1945 signaled the end of the war.

Page 47

1. In 1900, there were 1 billion, 600 million people in the world.
2. In 1 A.D., there were 300 million people in the world.
3. The world population is increasing.
4. Students should say that population growth was faster after 1900.

Page 48

1. The main energy source in the world is petroleum.
2. The world gets 25% of its energy needs from coal.
3. Nuclear energy fills about 6% of the world's energy needs.
4. The world gets the least energy from geothermal, solar, and wind sources.
5. Answers will vary.

Page 49

1. The United States had a higher rate of unemployment in 1975.
2. Canada had a higher rate of unemployment in 1985.
3. From 1990 to 1995, unemployment in Canada increased.
4. From 1990 to 1995, unemployment in the United States was steady. It did not increase or decrease.
5. Answers will vary but should include evidence from the graph.

Page 50

1. Spain had the greatest area of colonization in North America and Central America.
2. In eastern South America, Portugal had the greatest area of colonization.
3. The distance from the southern tip of South America to the Equator is about 5,000 miles.

Page 51

1. A
2. D
3. C
4. A

Page 52

1. The Polos set out from Venice, Italy, in 1271.
2. Venice is about 6,000 miles from Shang-tu.
3. The map suggests that Polo traveled south first, then turned west toward Venice.

Page 53

Answers may vary. Accept reasonable responses.

1. The audience for this poster would be workers in the United States.
2. The largest word on the poster is "Warning!," and it causes people to pay attention to the consequences of their work.
3. The main idea of the poster is that carelessness on the job in the United States can cause danger to the soldiers overseas.
4. If a person is careless in the workplace, a soldier might suffer as a result.

Page 54

1. The photograph was taken at the North Pole on April 7, 1909.
2. Answers will vary.

Page 55

1. No, the cartoon says that Matthew Henson planted the flag at the North Pole and that Peary was ill and confined to a sledge.
2. Answers will vary.

Page 56

1. The lake behind the dam represents our natural resources.
2. The leak in the dam represents the waste of those natural resources.
3. The main idea is that we need to be careful with the use of our natural resources or we may run out. Answers about effectiveness will vary.

Page 57

1. The man in the cartoon is Uncle Sam, who represents the United States.
2. Uncle Sam is running to war while peace tries to hold him back, but Uncle Sam's coattails rip, so he is free to go to war.
3. A piece of paper in his pocket suggests he is upset about the sinking of the *Maine*.
4. Answers will vary but might suggest that anger over events can

cause a nation to go to war.

Page 58
1. The Korean War started when North Korea invaded South Korea in June 1950.
2. The United States and the United Nations sided with South Korea in the war. China sided with North Korea.
3. A cease-fire is a halt in hostilities. A cease-fire was signed in July 1953.

Page 59
1. The prewar boundary between North Korea and South Korea was the 38th Parallel.
2. During the first few months of the war, North Korea seemed to be winning because it had taken over much of South Korea.
3. During the fall of 1950, South Korea seemed to be winning because it had taken over much of North Korea.

Page 60
1. none
2. got larger
3. Answers will vary but should suggest the economy improved.

Page 61
1. It was confronted with serious economic problems.
2. The Mexican leaders had no experience, and the many revolutions and changes in leadership made the situation more unstable.
3. The chart and the last sentence of the text excerpt suggest that

Mexico's economy was improving.

Page 62
1. The United States invested the most money in the Mexican economy.
2. Answers may vary but should suggest that stable leadership and increased foreign investment helped the economy to improve.
3. Answers will vary.

Page 64
1. Columbus's ships first sailed south along the coast of Africa before turning west.
2. Columbus and his ships never reached the mainland of the United States.
3. Columbus returned to Spain in 1493.

Page 65
1. Land was first sighted shortly after midnight on October 12, 1492.
2. Columbus first stepped ashore in the New World on Friday, October 12, 1492.
3. He says the island was green, with streams and fruit. The people were friendly and generous.

Page 66
1. Answers will vary.
2. Answers will vary but should use evidence from the journal entry and the illustration.

Page 67
1. 1493
2. 1498
3. 1502
4. 1506
5. Answers will vary.

Page 71
1. Northern Egypt

around Giza had the most pyramids.
2. Many temples and monuments were located near the Valley of the Kings.
3. The Sahara covers most of Egypt.
4. The Red Sea lies to the east of Egypt.
5. The Mediterranean Sea lies to the north of Egypt.

Page 72
1. The Egyptians made ink by mixing soot and vegetable gum.
2. A person read a papyrus book by holding it with both hands, and unrolling it at one end while rolling it up at the other end.
3. Answers will vary.

Page 73
1. Ra the sun-god was regarded as the greatest of the Egyptian gods.
2. Answers may vary but should suggest that the phoenix's rebirth after death represented the Egyptian belief in an afterlife.

Page 74
1. Osiris and Isis were the parents of Pasht.
2. Pasht was pictured with the head of a cat and the body of a young woman.
3. Answers will vary but should suggest the Egyptians worshiped cats because they believed that by doing so, they were also worshiping Pasht.

Page 75
1. The Great Pyramid

of Cheops is 480 feet high.
2. The pyramid is placed so that its four sides face the four points of the compass.
3. The Sphinx has the body of a lion and the head of a man. It is 90 feet long and 74 feet high.

Page 76
1. Answers will vary but should suggest the Sphinx has suffered from weathering.
2. Answers will vary.
3. Answers will vary.

Page 77
1. Howard Carter, assisted by Lord Carnarvon, discovered the tomb of King Tutankhamen in 1922.
2. The tomb contained a throne, gem-studded chariots, alabaster vases, dried meats, furniture, and gold and jewels.
3. Answers will vary but should suggest the Egyptians placed the items in the tomb for the use of the king in the afterlife.

Page 78
1. The photograph was taken at the opening of King Tutankhamen's tomb in the Valley of the Kings in November 1922.
2. Answers will vary.
3. Answers will vary.

Page 81
1. The photograph was taken at the Great Wall of China east of Nan-Kow Pass in 1900.

2. The horsemen in the picture are members of Troop L of the 6th U.S. Cavalry.
3. The photograph shows the size of the wall and how the wall runs up hills rather than around them.

Page 82
1. One third of the able-bodied men of China worked to build the Great Wall.
2. The foundation is made of stone set in mortar, and the rest is constructed of bricks.
3. The wall is 15 to 30 feet tall, depending on the terrain.

Page 83
1. The foundation of the Great Wall is five feet thick.
2. The watchtowers were used to house soldiers.
3. Answers may vary but should suggest the wall was built to control who entered China.

Page 86
1. Patience Kershaw worked in the mine about 12 hours a day.
2. Patience was a hurrier in the mine.
3. Patience moved over 2,000 pounds of coal a day.
4. Answers may vary but should suggest Patience was not educated and that she did not like working in the mine.
5. Answers will vary.

Page 87
1. Robert North started working in the mine when he was 7 years old.
2. He suffered cuts, backaches, and hip aches.
3. If he did not do his job well, he would be beaten.
4. Answers will vary.

Page 88
1. The smallest children of four, five, and seven years were usually hired to open and close the doors of the mine.
2. Trappers did not have hard work, but they had to sit in the dark without much to do for 12 hours a day.
3. The coal was moved around in large tubs that usually did not have wheels. They were pushed or pulled across the rough floor of the mine.
4. Usually, older children and half-grown girls were hired to move the coal.
5. The hurriers and drawers had to pull or push the tubs up steep inclines and through tunnels that were usually no more than three feet high.

Page 89
1. The women carried the coal in sacks that were attached to straps around their foreheads. They had to carry the sacks, which weighed over a hundred pounds, up and down ladders and through low tunnels.
2. Answers will vary.
3. Answers will vary.

Page 90
1. The 1842 Mines Act said females and boys under 10 years old could no longer work underground.
2. The act did not place any limits on the number of hours worked.
3. Answers will vary.

Page 93
1. Turkey and Bulgaria were on the side of the Central Powers in World War I.
2. France and Italy were on the side of the Allies in World War I.
3. Students should name two of the following: Spain, Switzerland, Denmark, Norway, and Sweden.
4. Answers will vary.

Page 94
1. In later wars, most soldiers did not ride horses. They drove in jeeps or trucks instead.
2. Answers will vary.

Page 95
1. After the torpedo struck the *Lusitania*, first a huge explosion occurred, with a large cloud of smoke. Then a second explosion occurred, and the superstructure and bridge were torn apart. The ship began to list and sank immediately.
2. Great confusion arose on the ship, and some of the lifeboats were lowered. Many people ended up in the water.
3. Answers will vary.
4. Answers will vary.

Page 96
1. According to the cartoon, President Wilson's reason for seeking a declaration of war was the sinking of American ships and the loss of American lives.
2. Answers will vary.

Page 97
1. The Allies had more soldiers than the Central Powers.
2. About 4,888,891 Allied soldiers were killed in World War I.
3. The Central Powers had more civilians killed.
4. Answers may vary but should suggest that the Allies had greater losses in real numbers.

Page 98
1. Answers will vary.
2. Owen portrays the gas attack as being under a green sea, and the man without a mask is drowning.
3. Answers will vary but might suggest the poem is against war.
4. Answers will vary.

Page 99
1. The poster tries to make people support the war by buying victory bonds.
2. Answers will vary.
3. Answers will vary.

Page 102
1. The Space Race began in 1957 when the Soviet Union launched its first satellite, *Sputnik*.
2. Soviet cosmonaut Yuri Gagarin was the first person in space.

Voices: World History, SV 9781419036392

3. Soviet cosmonaut Valentina Tereshkova was the first woman in space.
4. The United States won the Space Race in 1969 by landing men on the moon.
5. Answers will vary.

Page 103
1. President Kennedy wanted to land a man on the moon by the end of the 1960s.
2. Answers will vary.
3. Answers will vary.

Page 104
1. Answers will vary. The actual measurements of the *Friendship 7* capsule were 9.5 feet (2.9 m) tall, with a maximum diameter of 6.25 feet (1.9 m).
2. Answers will vary.
3. Answers will vary.

Page 105
1. The first woman in space was Russian cosmonaut Valentina Tereshkova.
2. Her flight was launched on June 16, 1963.
3. She says that once one goes into space, the earth seems much smaller and more fragile.

Page 106
1. According to the article, the environment on the moon would be bleak, with no atmosphere.
2. The author says people want to fly in space because people have always been compelled to explore the unknown and to overcome obstacles.
3. Answers will vary.

Page 107
1. The Eagle was the name of the lunar module that actually landed on the moon. The eagle represents the United States.
2. Answers will vary.

Page 108
1. Answers will vary.
2. Answers will vary.

Page 109
1. 22 hours
2. 67 hours
3. *Apollo 17*
4. Each later spaceship stayed on the moon's surface longer.
5. Answers will vary.

Page 112
1. The Berlin Wall was erected overnight on August 13, 1961.
2. The Berlin Wall was torn down on November 9, 1989.
3. The first person was shot on August 24, 1961, and the last person was shot on February 6, 1989.
4. Answers will vary.

Page 113
1. President Kennedy delivered this speech in Berlin, West Germany, on June 26, 1963.
2. Answers will vary but should suggest that a system that must entrap its people is not very successful.
3. Answers will vary but might suggest that the Wall separated friends, neighbors, and family members.

Page 114
1. Answers will vary but might suggest that

they did not like living in a dictatorship.
2. Answers will vary.

Page 115
1. President Reagan made this speech in Berlin, West Germany, on June 12, 1987.
2. The scar he is referring to is the Berlin Wall. It is like an injury to the city of Berlin.
3. President Reagan said that if Mr. Gorbachev wanted peace, prosperity, and more democracy, he should tear down the Wall.

Page 116
1. Czechoslovakia was a Communist country in 1989.
2. Students should name one of the following: Italy, West Germany, Austria, Denmark, Greece, Turkey, Albania.
3. In 1989, most of Eastern Europe was Communist.
4. Answers will vary.

Page 117
1. The photograph was taken at the Brandenburg Gate in the Berlin Wall on November 9, 1989.
2. Answers will vary.
3. Answers will vary.

Answer Key
Voices: World History, SV 9781419036392